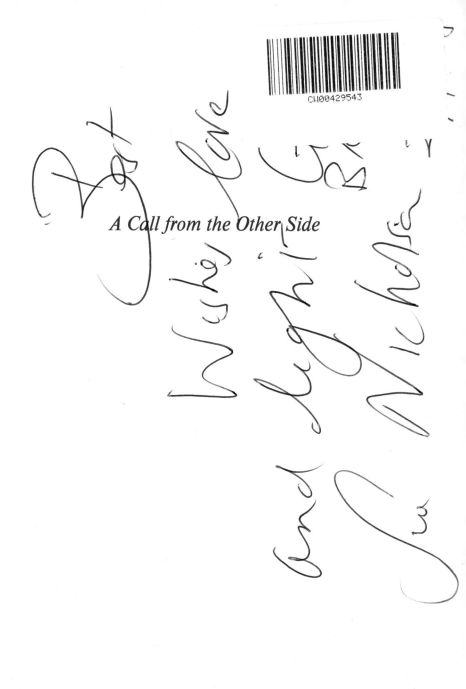

A Call from the Other Side

A Call from the Other Side

The life story of Psychic Medium Sue Nicholson

**As told to and written by
Sue Murray**

A Message from Sue

Many years ago Spirit told me that in time I would write a book about my life.

"You will write this book," Spirit said, *"to bring clarification and understanding for the reader, that no matter what hardship they may endure, there is an underlying universal plan for all in each life that they live. By learning to trust that all experiences in life are for a purpose then the most wonderful, and enlightening Spiritual path will open up.*

The book will be written when your mother and father have passed over because there will be things in the book that some of your family will not understand. Please, we ask you not to hesitate but to go ahead with this book. Someone, somewhere, will be helped as they may find themselves in a situation just like you have experienced, and they will learn how to move through it and achieve anything in life they set out to do."

All my life I have known there is more to our existence than the physical life we live. I have always been surrounded by passed loved ones, angels and entities in another dimension, all of which I call Spirit. To me Spirit is a higher universal energy that provides us with wisdom, guidance and perception that can assist us with everyday issues in our life and beyond. Depending on the situation I see, hear or feel Spirit and this comes through in a thought process producing very quick simple, positive and uncomplicated answers.

"You are never alone. We always walk with you." These words I hear from Spirit often.

Spirit has been the support I have needed to be able to move through the many tests that I have been put through in this lifetime. Even my husband, family and close friends do not know of all that I have experienced. I have recalled to the best of my ability and also with the help of Spirit the stories of my life that I feel have made me who I am today. In this book I have not set out to hurt anyone, but by reflecting on my past I am now able to accept that all this learning has empowered me to do the work I was destined to do.

Spirit has been with me through the whole process of recording, writing and completing this book. The true stories that are told from my work are here not because I remember them from a client's session but because they have been channelled through again to me to give clarity around the concepts contained within the book. When Spirit has done this their words and thoughts are *in Italics*.

We are all able to communicate with the other side but for me to have such a direct and clear line and to be privileged to do the work that I do, I feel tremendously blessed.

Prologue: The Contract

"I signed what?" I anxiously asked Spirit.

"You signed a contract with us."

The whole room seemed to be filled with this most powerful energy and I heard the words again.

"You signed a contract with us. A contract, you are unable to give up!"

"What contract? I cannot remember signing a contract?"

"You signed a contract with us, well before you were born to this Earth. It stated that you would work for us unconditionally, that you would give messages from us here in Spirit, to those people who we would send to you and that this contract would only be completed when you passed over. This is your life time's work of service."

I knew it was the highest of beings and this definitive reply from Spirit, who were once again guiding and supporting me, deeply touched my whole being. It was in response to my desperate thoughts that I had, had that morning, and actually the same thoughts I did have many mornings as I awoke; I am living a lie and any minute now I will be found out. I am just making it all up. How could I see past loved ones? How could I hear the words of Spirit from the other side? How could I actually feel and know how someone has passed over? How could I, Sue Nicholson be able to do all of this? These intense moments of desperation continued to haunt me as the gift of mediumship increased and more people asked of my services.

"Spirit, why then has my life been so hard, if the contract was already signed as to what I was to do this lifetime?" I asked, "Why did you put me through all these experiences?"

"You are and will be working with many people, who have had many varied and difficult experiences themselves. How can you walk in their shoes when you have never walked in them yourself? All these experiences have been there for you to learn and grow from."

"So every hardship that I have endured has been for a reason?"

"Look at it this way. Every time another testing experience comes up, it is like another exam for you. You can either fail it or move through it, gaining the highest marks you possibly can. Through this you will develop empathy with the people you serve."

Spirit then proceeded to show me what it is like on the other side before we come to earth. They showed me hundreds of people lining up and there I was in one of those lines.

"You are in pure form," they said.

"What do you mean pure form?"

"You are just a pure white Spiritual energy with no 'overcoat' on. You have completely healed from past life times and you carry no emotional ties as you line up to begin a new physical life. The line that you are in is the line of all those

souls that have contracted to work with Spirit to bring through messages of guidance. These messages will assist those who are seeking to understand their existence on the earth plane. You are seeing yourself in the queue choosing the family that you will be born into for the life lessons that will give you the strength to do the work that is required of you. Here on the other side we look for certain people-recruits that under all conditions will continue to work for us.

Over many lifetimes you have lived as many different people, and have learnt many and varied lessons. Free will has always been there for you, and you could have walked away from your contract this lifetime, but you have known in the deepest part of your soul that this is your life's work. This is what you were born this lifetime to do so do this well as this will be your last contract on earth. Your learning will be complete."

Contents

The Existence I have Chosen

I propped the pillows up around my mother to ease her pain, as she lay in bed in the last few weeks of her life. Our eyes locked on each other as I sat down on the side of the bed. In this moment we were suddenly transformed into another era and we were both seeing a past lifetime that we had shared together. I became her mother and she my daughter and we were dressed in dirty ragged, sack-like clothes. Spirit told me the date was 1839 and we lived in the pauper's area of London. I was full of anger and I was treating her with much disdain as I dragged her along the street shouting abuse at her. Then it was gone. I jumped back and she moved back on her pillow.

"I understand," was all I could say.

My mother was lost for words and looked at me as if to say, "Where did we both go, what happened there?"

This past life was showing us what I was and what she was and that we had come back together in this lifetime to bring balance and understanding. By being placed in each others shoes I at least could reconcile why this lifetime had developed as it did. Even though my mother had shared no previous knowledge of past lives I think she instinctively knew what we had both experienced. I believe now she had the ability to see Spirit just as I do.

A look of kindness and love appeared on her face. It was a look that I had never seen before.

"I wouldn't have known what to have done without you, if you hadn't come home. Thank you," she said to me.

To hear my mother say these words was what I had been waiting all my life to hear. Both our lives from this moment on were totally transformed as we had found some peace between us, before she passed over.

I had been back in England now for two weeks, tending my mother as she lay dying of lung cancer. All her life she had been a passive smoker and it had finally caught up with her. When I had received the call from my father, I knew in my heart that I had to go back and say goodbye. I had to put aside my feelings of anger towards my mother and father that had built up over all these years. Spirit had spoken to me and told me,

"It is time to visit your mother one last time."

The trip from New Zealand had been long, and I had many hours to think about my parents, my life, how it had unfolded and the gift that I was blessed with. Steve, my husband had not wanted me to return home to England as he regularly saw me suffering from the lack of contact and the unloving words that were spoken when I did contact them. He could not understand how I would want to travel all the way back to England to visit my parents when they obviously had not shown the same concern for me all these years. I heard his voice ringing in my ears,

"Why are you going back when she treated you so badly? Can you not just leave it alone and get on with your life?"

Even though he was so against me going home to see my dying mother, he supported me in getting the money so I could return. It put our family and finances under tremendous pressure to find some closure in my life. Spirit has always been with me and over the years I have learnt to trust and follow the guidance that I received. I always knew that I would be guided home when the time was right.

When you have been treated cruelly and have had problems with those closest to you and that person is dying, there is just something inside of you wanting to see them one more time. Maybe you hope there will be one kind word, a smile, something. Maybe, there is a glimmer of hope that you will finally receive some love and acceptance that you have craved for all of your life. Maybe you will find forgiveness.

After six weeks, my mother still had not passed. It was time to return home to New Zealand as I was pining for my beloved Steve and my three beautiful daughters. I had arrived in England with very little money and my father insisted I pay board while I was living with them. I had found a job but I just seemed to be working and not really spending a lot of time with my mother. Nearly all of the money I earned was given to my father and even though I had to again suffer my father's meanness, going to see my mother had been the right thing to do. There was now a new unspoken feeling between us and I was finding some forgiveness in my heart. I felt I could now return home and begin to move on with my life back in New Zealand.

I had been home for only a short while when I awoke one morning to find this most beautiful violet mist swirling around the room. It was the sign that my mother had finally passed. Her name was Violet and as I was saying "that's my mother," the phone rang and it was England telling me that my mother had gone. I see her often when she visits me from the other side. She always looks in her twenties and is dressed in clothes of that era. I asked her once,

"Why are you dressed in those clothes and you look so young when you come through?"

"You can be whatever you want here on the other side. You can wear what you want; you can be whatever age you want to be. I have chosen the time I was the most happiest in my life," she replied.

With this new beginning in my life and with Spirit's help I have learned more about what forgiveness is.

"It is not the physical nature of the experience that you are forgiving, it is the forgiving of the soul of the person. To truly understand and demonstrate forgiveness to another person is one of the greatest leanings you can have as a human being."

When I heard and understood this Universal Law from Spirit, over time I have been able to detach and let go of the anger that had built in my life as a result of what I had experienced as a young person. Many times since my mother has passed, I have thanked her for the wisdom and the life lessons that she has given me as I am only where I am today through these experiences which I signed a contract to go through with.

* * * *

We choose our families that we are to be born into for the lessons we are to learn this life time. Sometimes we are guided to choose families with wealth, high society and good education. I was guided to choose to be born into the world of hardship and negativity, where every day of my early life would be a struggle. Every day would be a test but it would eventually form the foundation of strength that I would require to live and complete the life I was contracted to do.

It was the height of summer when I was born on the 31st of July 1954 and given the name of Susan Violet Bagley. The first time my mother saw me, as I was handed to her from the midwife, she was horror shocked.

"What is the matter with this baby? Where is her arm? I can't see her arm!" my mother shouted in disbelief.

There was anger in her voice as she had not wanted another baby and this obviously, problematic one was going to add more stress into a life that was already difficult.

Hurriedly, the midwife reached for me, and took me back. She realised that she had missed putting my arm through the night gown's armhole and my arm was trapped behind my back. Quickly, she righted the situation and handed me back to my mother. My mother continued to stare at me.

"Your daughter has eczema. It can be treated," the nurse tried to cheer her up.

This moment of my mother's anxiety was the start of how I was going to be harshly treated for the rest of my childhood. The bond between mother and baby never formed.

I was the second of three children, a brother three years older, and a sister, five years younger. The industrial area on the outskirts of Birmingham, England was my home for the first eight years of my life. We were extremely poor and we lived in a very old house. Coronation Street looked like a palace, compared with where I lived.

To get to my house, you went to the end of the street and through an archway into a shared yard with cobbled stones where there were twelve houses connected together in a row. Factories sandwiched us and not one house had a garden or its own play space. The windows of our house faced towards the huge brick walls of the steel press factory that worked twenty four hours a day. All night and all day the banging from the machines did not stop. As a young child I would often try and decipher if it was the sound of the factory or was it 'somebody' in the house.

The house was tiny with the front door opening

straight into the front living room which contained a small settee, a couple of chairs and an old box TV as well as the kitchen sink. The kitchen, which was basically a cupboard, could just fit in a cooker. We had no hot running water in the house. There was a winding staircase from the living room going up to the only bedroom where my mother, Violet, and my father, Harry, slept. I slept up in the very small attic, which I shared with my brother.

From the kitchen there was a little doorway with stairs going right the way down into the cellar where my father kept all his carpentry tools amongst the coal. Outside under the front living room window was a grate that allowed the coalman to empty his coal straight into the cellar. I used to spend many hours down here playing as it was quite mysterious and my family did not disturb me. I loved the smell of the wood and the coal and no matter how damp, cold and scary it was at times, it was a space of my own.

I had a small red plastic telephone and this would come down into the cellar with me. It became my lifeline whenever I wasn't feeling happy inside.

"Hello, hello, are you there?" I would say into the hand piece. Then I would hear voices on the other end. It was Spirit and they would begin to tell me,

"Remember, you are a special little girl, with a special job to do."

After this reassurance they would talk very quickly to me. I listened but did not understand it as they were laying down wisdom teachings, which I am now able to call upon. This was our way of communicating together and Spirit's way of supporting and teaching me.

We didn't have a toilet or bathroom in the house. I would have to walk to these communal toilets that everyone shared. There were two old cold concrete blocks of three toilets for the twelve families to use. The block that our family used, had a hole in the wall that I could look through and see other people and no doubt people looked through at me as well. Sometimes my friend, from the next door house would go to the toilet at the same time as me and we would sit there for ages having wonderful conversations together. No one could afford toilet paper so, my grandmother cut up newspaper, and hung it on the wall on a butcher's hook for all to use.

In the mornings I would get dressed and then go to the toilet. I would hold on so tightly all night as there was no way I could go out into the yard when it was dark. Winter brought more difficulty with going to the toilet as the yard would be covered in thick snow and it would be extremely cold. Sometimes I would wet the bed and I dreaded this as I knew I would be in big trouble with my mother.

My father used to work hard as a Carpenter all week for very little money. There were no luxuries in our house such as a phone or a car and a treat was rare. It was an extremely hard life and Birmingham, like most cities in England was still suffering the consequences of World War Two. There was very little joy or laughter in the house and I felt my parents were very unhappy people.

Fridays became the day I would dread. Dad would come home from work and start getting ready to go out. As soon as he went out the door my mother would then begin to take it out on me. She would get into a rage, and I would be petrified. I used to sit up in the corner by the fireplace and cower as she went berserk.

"Keep out of her way," I would silently say to myself as every negative thought about me, my mother could conjure up, came out of her mouth.

"You are no good. You are ugly. Nobody will ever like you. You will have no friends and you will never do any good in this world."

These words used to echo through every part of my being. I would close my eyes and not move, too scared to look anywhere, hoping she would stop.

Then I would hear Spirit whisper into my other ear, *"Don't listen to her, don't listen."* I would then separate from my mother's energy and block off any more nasty words.

When my father was out he would be drinking with his three brothers and often he would not come back until Sunday night. Even if he did come back on Saturday morning, the atmosphere in the house was horrible and he would get ready to go out again. All my mother could see was another weekend of being left alone with young children and their precious money being spent. I never saw my father hit my mother but there were terrible rows.

One Saturday morning he came home and he was covered in blood and I asked him,

"What's happened to you Dad?"

And he said, "I fell out of a car." I wanted to believe this was true, but I knew it wasn't as he was always in fights.

My father had a very sad and unhappy childhood and he had grown up in an incredibly dysfunctional family. When I was older, my grandmother Louise, my father's mother, shared with me about my father's life. My father had endured a violent upbringing with a lot of abuse. His father, who was an alcoholic, had grown into an extremely violent person and he often used to physically abuse my grandmother. Once when she was pregnant my grandfather broke her arm and leg, kicked her in the stomach and chucked her out in the snow. She was very ill and lost the baby. Eventually she left him and went to live with one of her daughters.

When my grandmother was in hospital recovering, all the children were palmed out to different homes. My father, who was seven years old, was taken to live on a farm with a couple who had no children. He would be locked up in a small cupboard under the stairs in the dark and was abused. My father told me once in a drunken stupor "I am afraid of the dark you know." This was the only time he ever shared anything personal about growing up. He had to work on the farm and was hardly fed and I am sure this episode in his life, mentally disturbed him. A picture I saw showed him to be very thin and he was suffering from malnutrition. When my grandmother started to get the children back, she told me that of all her children, Harry my father was in the most terrible state. Eventually there were seven children, three girls and four boys and my father was the second eldest of the boys.

The cruelty from the father was bestowed onto the boys of the family. A regular night of entertainment was each boy had to fight the other until blood was drawn. If blood wasn't drawn they would get strapped with a big leather belt. This was my grandfather's fun and his way of toughening the boys up. My grandfather died in hospital by himself as an alcoholic being disowned by the majority of his family. My father was the only family member that visited him but we children never did.

At only seventeen my father forged his age, enlisted with his brothers and joined the Royal Navy to go to the Second World War to get away. My father used to take photographs of everybody and anything. He had a huge box full of photos and once when I found the box, I saw a picture of him during the war in Malaysia standing next to many dead mutilated corpses. I will never forget that photo. He caught me looking at it and he shouted at me,

"Don't ever look at this again!"

"What is it?" I asked.

"You don't want to know," was all he could say.

My mother met my father when she was twenty seven and my dad twenty three. He was a singer in a pub and he tried to impress her but she was having none of it. There weren't many eligible men around after the war and not wanting to be left on the shelf she did finally succumb and they were married. They were not married long when she had my brother, then a number of miscarriages and then me. My mother tried to be brave and do the best she could in very difficult and testing circumstances.

To cope, my mother developed two sides to herself. There was one; the outside face, everyone thought Vi was this person, kind and caring and living a very normal life. Then there was the Vi behind closed doors, where she vented her built up anger and hatred to those around her, especially me. This always intensified when my father went out. I believe she was very depressed.

As a child you are not seeing the bigger picture of your parent's early and present experiences in life. You cannot understand why your mother and father are treating you in these ghastly ways and you come to believe that everything is your fault and that you are always doing something wrong. Most of my whole memory of my childhood was devoid of happy family times and I came to learn that this is how life was going to be for me.

Often when I was upstairs in my attic bedroom desperate and crying for somebody to come and pick me up, this figure would appear, dressed in very old clothes. There was a window opposite my cot and when the curtains were not drawn properly, the lights from the factory next door would shine through the gap. As I looked at him, he seemed very real.

"Shoosh, shoosh, it is all right," he would say gently to me.

I would quietly lie down and go to sleep.

He came to me often to soothe me. This was my first memory of seeing Spirit.

"I have seen this man," I said pointing to a very old picture of the man who visited me in my bedroom at night. Dad loved all his photos, many he had taken himself. He would spread them out all out over the floor so we could look at them.

"I have seen him," I excitedly said again.

My father shouted at me,

"You would never have seen him that's impossible. He died a long time ago. He is your great grandfather!"

I knew it was the man that I saw in my bedroom at night.

My grandparents, on my mother's side, and their daughter, my aunty Ivy, unmarried and fourteen years my mother's junior, lived three doors away in the same group of houses. When I was at my grandmother's, she always seemed to be in the lounge rolling pastry and making apple pies on the dining table as the kitchen was too small to work in. She would always have a lovely big apron on that she tied round the back and then tied around the front. I would learn to roll pastry and cook with her as we sang and laughed together and listened to her old boxed radio. She always had time for me, and she was extremely kind. My aunty and grandmother were my salvation.

Whenever I had an upset at home, during the day, I would quietly creep out of the house and go down there for some comfort and support. They knew I was treated unkindly by my mother and father, but they never intervened to my knowledge and did what they could for me. After a particularly bad time of wetting my bed repeatedly I took refuge in their house, fearing retribution from my mother.

I heard the knock on the door and my mother came in. Quickly I went and hid behind the lounge chair. My mother accusingly said to my aunty,

"Where is she, is she here?"

My aunty suspecting what I had done said,

"No I haven't seen her, she is not here."

Then, for whatever reason I jumped out from behind the big chair and said,

"Boo! I am here."

This was not the reaction my mother wanted. She went mad, grabbed me by the collar and marched me home. My mother had this look on her face that always frightened me and when you saw this look, you knew it was time to do what she wanted. You did not disobey. I was banned from my grandmother's house for what seemed like an eternity.

My mother used to be quite horrible to her mother, my grandmother, at times and I would wonder "why are you talking to her like that, why are you so mean?" The fear on my grandmother's face at times told me she was also frightened of my mother but I never said anything as I was not to answer back.

Grandmother Florence had grown up in the workhouse. She had no brothers and sisters and she did not know her parents. She was very capable at what she did as she had learnt to work from a very young age. My grandfather was Jewish and he changed his name from Smitaman to Smitherman. Even though I spent a lot of time at their house, I never learnt any stories of either of their early lives.

When I didn't go to my grandmothers, I found other people in the neighbourhood to visit. I was quite a popular little girl with the neighbours, but I was very, very shy. There was a lady next door her name was Mrs Ashford, Oh Spirit are telling me *"her first name, it was Gerry, Gertrude."* She didn't have any children and was married to a man who had two grown up boys. I was very small and very slender and her big Alsatian dog frightened me, as I am sure it was bigger than me. Mrs Ashford would take me out for the whole day shopping and on Sundays sometimes, she would take me to her sisters where I would have food that I never saw in our house, such as pears and cream. One thing my mother always taught me was to be polite, give and always offer to help, so I often would do chores for Mrs Ashford. Mrs Ashford would say, "have a biscuit for helping me" and she would give me biscuits. It didn't matter that they were always old and stale and I would eat them quickly, as a biscuit in my house was a very rare treat.

Mrs Ashford was a lovely lady. She seemed to really care for me and she enjoyed having me visit. Often she would say, "will you dance for me?" and I used to spin around and pretend I was a ballerina. Coming home from Mrs Ashford's one day feeling so happy I wanted to show my mother, how I could spin like a ballerina. My mother was ironing, I was only four and not yet at school.

"Mummy, one day I am going to be a ballerina," I said as I spun around. I then stood up on my toes to show her what I could do but she wasn't interested.

"You will never do that; you will never ever be a ballerina," my mother told me. I cried and cried that night as that was the end of my dream as I had grown to believe everything my mother said about me.

Carrying out everyday tasks was always a struggle for my mother living in this complex of houses and often whole days were taken up with what we see today as simple tasks. We didn't have a washhouse, as that was also communal for the twelve houses. It was wash day every Monday for our family and this was the only day that we had in the week. I would lie in bed and hear the alarm go off. The next door neighbour would organise the lines for the washing in the yard and then would knock at the upstairs bedroom window with the prop just to make sure my mother was up. She would go to the wash house to start stacking up the wood to get the fire going to boil up the washing and all day she would do little else.

Every Saturday was bath day and so out would come the big tin bath to be put in front of the fire for my brother and me to be washed. Luckily there was no carpet, only lino as the bath was often knocked over by my brother as he tried to fit his ever increasing body into the small bath.

Sometimes when we had a shilling to spare we went to the public bath house. Men and boys on one side, women and girls on the other side. I would bath with Mum.

"Shut your eyes," she would say.

I would have to shut my eyes so I couldn't see her and then hop in first. I would sit with my back to the middle of the bath. When she was sure I could not see her and my eyes were still shut, she would take her clothes off and get in. She would sit with her back to me. I would wash myself and be very careful not to turn around and catch a glimpse of her.

When it was time to get out, I would have to shut my eyes again and she would get out. She would hurriedly dry and dress herself. Then I was allowed to get out. I never did see her naked.

My Aunty Ivy would also come with us. One day my aunty discovered body lice in the bath when she went in and that was the end to our public baths.

The problem now became, where do we go for a bath each week? Luckily my uncle offered their house and so each Saturday we would bus over for our weekly wash. My aunty would fill the bath up and we would all have turns. I was always last. It was filthy with all scum around the sides and I would have great difficulty even getting into the well-used water. Sometimes I just could not get in and I would run the sink next to the bath and just get a flannel. I used to splash the bathwater to assure my mother and everyone else that I was actually in the bath.

My mother would yell out to me,
"Susan, are you in the bath?"
I would call back,
"Yes mum," and splash the water a bit louder.

When I would come out, she would grab me around my neck to see if I was clean and to ensure that I had been telling the truth.

Sue with her mother in the backyard with archway and toilet block in Birmingham, 1956.

Sue with her brother Allan and his friend sitting on the doorstep, Birmingham, 1957.

Sue aged 3 years in the backyard, Birmingham, 1957.

*A neighbour and her brother's friend in the backyard,
Birmingham, 1958.*

Mrs Ashford with her dog, 1958.

Sensing Energies

My mother's life was harsh and often she became pregnant. My father did not know how to care for my mother as he had no role model as a child. This night even though my mother was poorly and had gone to bed to rest as she was spotting heavily, my father still went out drinking with his brothers. I quietly went into the bedroom to see how she was and there was my mother lying in a pool of blood, extremely grey looking and barely able to speak. I didn't know what it was but she was haemorrhaging from a miscarriage and there was nobody home to help her. I ran to get my grandmother and she was able to take care of the situation and get her to hospital.

Not long after this my mum was pregnant again, this time with my sister. I was four years old. My mother was not well during this pregnancy again and her legs would swell up with varicose veins. Out would come the bowl of hot water and I would massage her feet as she soaked them, then dry her feet and put talcum powder on them. In these later years when I massage feet, they are my favourite part of the body and I am sure this comes from past lives in Egypt.

Mum had also begun a job in one of the factories, just over the back from our house, to clean the factory office after everyone had left for the day. She began at 6 o'clock in the early evening and I was taken with her. The office became a wonderful playground for me and I would swing around and around on the swivel chairs and play on the telephone switch board, clicking all the knobs up and down. I pretended I was an office worker and this became the only thing I wanted to do when I grew up.

"I am going to work on a typewriter one day," I often said and I would pick up the carbon and smell it and go off in my own little dream world.

"Stop swinging on that chair. Leave that telephone alone," my mother would shout at me and quickly I was brought back into reality.

"They will know when they come in what you have been doing because the chair won't be at the right height, you would have messed up all the switches and the papers won't be in the right places. I will lose my job. They will know you have been touching their things." There was always this fear with my mother.

I got into the habit of sitting in different people's chairs and sensing what sort of person they were. I was sensing each one's energies. I could tell if they were happy, sad and at times Spirit would tell me a little more about them and if something was going to happen to them. At the time I didn't understand the messages really or knew where I was getting this information from. I did know though never to tell my mother what I was getting.

As soon as the job was finished for the night, we

would rush back home so my mother could watch television. I would have to find my own way to bed, as she lost herself in the programme, having finally finished for the day.

The ability to sense people's energies interfered in my life and still does as people's energy is left behind on everything. Drinking out of certain cups when I was out became a real trial. I knew who had drunk out of them and if I didn't like their energy it was very difficult for me to use them. My mother used to get so angry with me because I was embarrassing her by not wanting to drink out of these cups when we went visiting. To get around it, I used to put my lips right inside it so my lips wouldn't touch the cups edges.

One Sunday afternoon when we were all at home Dad brought out these tiny little sherry glasses, he had got from somewhere for us to drink out of. We were allowed to put water into them, but there was something about these glasses. I didn't like the energy and so I put my lips right inside the glass which was now the habit. This time my lips became stuck, and they were getting bigger and bigger inside the glass. I looked like a fish. Unfortunately the glass had to be broken to get it off my lips and quite a commotion followed with my mother and father. It is extremely difficult to tell anyone what you are sensing and feeling when those around you have no concept of what it is you are experiencing. I was living this secret life.

It became even more difficult when people visited our house and I was able to sense if they were 'safe' to be near or not. There was a particular man who used to come to our house, he was a friend of my father's. We were instructed to call him uncle and every time he visited us we had to kiss him. There was something that was not nice about him and I would dread him coming. I would kiss him under threat and then I would turn around and quickly wipe my lips on my sleeve, hoping to rid myself of anything about him.

I treasured the time my mother finally went into hospital to await the birth of my sister. My favourite Aunty Ivy came along to look after us in the early evening before my father came home from work. She always spoiled me, and this time, was no exception. She bought my brother and me some fireworks. It was the fifth of November, Fireworks night. We didn't know ourselves, without the tight rein that our mother kept on us and we both went wild.

While my aunt was in the kitchen cooking dinner, my brother picked up the fireworks bag and threw all the fireworks into the fire. We had rockets going off in the living room, we had jumping jacks going off on the floor. The mat in front of the fireplace caught alight. I was screaming for it all to stop and went running out the house followed by my brother. He wasn't finished yet and out of his pocket came a box of these big matches called Bingles. For some reason he lit one and asked me to hold the lighted end. I was so naïve, frightened and totally intimidated by my big eight-year old brother, I did as he said. It stuck to my hand and burnt my hand. I was now screaming even more. Here we were with the house nearly burnt down, my hand with a badly burnt thumb, all outside trying to be comforted by my aunty. Luckily the house didn't burn down and unlike how my mother would have reacted, my aunty did not scold us.

Two nights later I was lying in bed there was a large knock on the door. It was a policeman.

"You need to come to the hospital now; your wife is being read the last rites!" I heard him telling my father. I didn't understand what that meant. He went to fetch my grandmother to look after us for the night. I remember asking my grandmother,

"What's the matter?"

"Nothing your mum is sick," she said.

The next morning my father came home, looking terrible. He had been with her all night. My mother had my sister and apparently my mother had haemorrhaged so badly that the blood she was losing had dripped right through the mattress and onto the floor. She was at death's door.

She stayed in hospital for a long time with my sister as they were both very ill. My sister had lung problems and was in an oxygen tent.

"Can I go and see my mother?" I constantly asked my grandmother Florence. I would always receive the same terse, negative reply, "No."

Finally they came home. However, for all the joy of my mother coming home, life changed for the worse. She had this new baby and if before I was not wanted, I certainly wasn't now. Her shouting increased and became more intense. Her near death experience had changed her for the worse.

One evening I was told to look after my baby sister, who was lying on the settee. My parents were in the small kitchen talking about what we would have that night for dinner. My new sister was tiny at four weeks old and so I sat on the end of the settee and began rubbing her feet, her toes, and her hands. My hands were drawn to her chest. I didn't know what I was doing but I heard a voice saying,

"You have to get her you have to get her now. You have to get your mother now!"

I didn't know why but I knew my sister was very ill.

I went into the kitchen and begun tugging on my mother's apron.

"The baby is sick, you have to come now," I said as I looked up at her.

"Just leave the baby alone; just get away from the baby!"

"No, no," I could hear the voices saying again.

I went back to the baby and put my hands on her.

The voices kept on saying, *"You have to get her now, you have to get her now."* I knew it was urgent by the way they were telling me.

I tried again with my mother. "You have to come now, the baby is very sick, you have to come now." She was annoyed with me but this time she finally listened to me.

When she did get to my sister, she was blue.

"What have you done? What have you done?" My mother began screaming not knowing what to do. My father ran down the road to the phone box to call for an ambulance. Everything was such a panic. I could hear the sirens of the ambulance in the distance getting closer and closer. The ambulance men quickly bundled her up and put her in the ambulance. No one thought she would survive. She stayed in hospital for a very long time as they tried to strengthen her lungs. I had done nothing except lay my hands on her and get help. She did survive.

Spirit Grows Stronger

As I was growing up, Spirit was there in all areas of my life.

"The car is red," I heard the words and saw the colour in my head.

"Its red," I said with certainty to my friends, as we all sat on the pavement outside the archway that formed the entrance to our yard, waiting for the next car to come around the corner. Within in a minute the next car arrived and it was red. The other children glared at me with frustration.

"We are not playing with you any more. You always get it right."

How could I explain to them, that I heard the answer in my head and I didn't know how I was doing it. I was never allowed to play the game of 'guessing the colour of the car before it comes around the corner' with the other children again.

When I went to school I had great difficulty forming friendships.

"Will you play with me?" I would ask other children. It was often 'no' and I was beginning to become affected by the constant rejection in my life with forming friendships.

Finally these three girls agreed to play with me and the game was hide and seek. They were going to hide and I would have to find them.

"Count to a hundred, before you come find us," they said as they ran away laughing.

Counting to a hundred was difficult for me. I obediently tried my best, as I always did what people told me to do. The boy's and girl's playgrounds were separated and we were not allowed to go over to the boy's area. I searched everywhere, and I remember standing there asking in my head, "Where are they? Where are they?"

"Go around by the back of the brick wall and into the boy's area and they are hiding down there," I heard Spirit say.

I ran off and it wasn't long before I found them.

"Got you!" I excitedly shouted.

They looked at me with such amazement and said,

"You are not playing with us again."

They couldn't understand how I had found them. As I didn't know how I was getting the answers I couldn't even think of not saying what I heard. That was the end of a new friendship beginning. These games certainly were teaching me that what I was hearing in my head was certainly going to happen. However as a child when you are repeatedly being told by other children that they do not want you to play with them, you withdraw into a shell and develop no sense of who you are or what you could be as a person. Continually you are striving to get somebody to like you, and to find someone who could be your friend. Who would actually like you begins to grow with each rejection.

Each night after having something to eat, I would sit on the pavement, under the archways hoping the other children would come out to play with me. One night a car pulled up and the man opened the door of his car and lent out.

"Would you like to go for a ride? Do you want a bottle of Coke?" He said to me.

We didn't have a car, so it all seemed very exciting, and for a bottle of Coke, well I was six years old and treats were wide and far between. The other children in the neighbourhood had not turned up and I was lonely. I got up on the seat of the car, my feet didn't even touch the floor. I was gone for a very long time, and it is all a blur now as to where he took me. He did drop me off a long way from my house. By this time it was starting to get dark. I looked around not knowing where I was. I silently asked for help to find my way home.

"Please angels, please show me how to get home."

I started walking and I was guided to the top of our road. There were my parents and all the neighbours out looking for me.

Someone shouted, "There she is!"

My parents began yelling and screaming at me,

"Where have you been? Where have you been?"

I couldn't understand what all the fuss was about.

"I've been for a ride in a car," I said, "He gave me a bottle of Coke." They kept on saying,

"Did he touch you anywhere?"

I didn't understand what they meant at the time. I

have searched my memory since but to no avail.

This curtailed my exploration of the neighbourhood and the freedom I had enjoyed. I was only allowed out if I stayed within the immediate yard. The old pram the relatives had given me was the vehicle I needed to begin taking the neighbours' cats and dogs for a ride. My favourite was a dog that had puppies. Carefully, I would wrap them in blankets, put them in the pram and walk them around. One day I couldn't find the pram. I hunted frantically everywhere in the neighbourhood. It wasn't anywhere to be found.

"My pram has gone," I said to my father with tears rolling down my face.

"I don't know where it is," my father angrily snapped back at me.

Over time I began to realise something about my father. Toys would be given to us one day and within a little while they wouldn't be there. He would always say,

"They've gone. I have given them to children who really want them," or "there's someone at work and he's got lots of kids."

After my pram had gone my cousin gave me her old three wheeler bike. It had a little tin boot at the back that you could unwind and put things in. I loved it. Now I had a new place to put the cats and dogs and wheel them about. One day I came to get my bike and my bike had gone. I was so upset and couldn't understand why these things were always being taken away from me. In time I realised he didn't give things away - he sold them for his beer money.

"When one grows up in a violent and abusive household,

you all have a moral duty to ensure the tape does not continue to play into the next generation. Somehow responsibility needs to be taken to break the cycle."

The tape was not being broken in my home or in some of the relatives'. Children have an instinctive ability to pick up on things about other children and for some, they will exert their own fragile power and bully these weaker children. I had always been taught not to say anything to other people out of turn, to be obedient and do what I was told without question. I never knew how to stand up for myself because, if I dared, I would receive the anger of my parents. An easy target was how I was seen by other children and crying and getting upset had become a way of life for me, not only at home, but also at school.

My Dad's oldest sister, Aunty Lou, owned a public house just around the corner from where we lived. My grandmother Louise lived there with them and looked after my cousin Janet when the public house was open and my aunty and uncle were busy working. Sometimes on a Sunday I would be sent over for the day. Janet who was four years older than me, and very spoilt, seemed to enjoy having some sort of power over me. She would boss me around and insisted that I do everything she told me to do. I had difficulty with what she wanted me to do one day and the next thing I knew she had grabbed me and was holding my head under the water in the big sink that she had filled up in the kitchen.

"Please let me up! Please let me up! Help me help me, please someone help me!" I screamed in my head.

Luckily my grandmother came in and saw what she

was doing to me.

"Let her go, Janet!" my grandmother yelled.

Janet developed an obviously mean streak in her and enjoyed picking on me. Was there something to sort out in this lifetime that we had carried through from a previous life? Was this karma?

It was a Sunday, just after Christmas when I was again sent to the public house to play. I hadn't been there long when Janet pulled out her doctor's bag to begin a game. She carefully opened it up. Out came the plastic toy syringe and into the end went a huge darning needle from my grandmothers sewing basket.

"Susan," she called me over. She sounded ever so nice and so over I went, hoping that she was going to play with me finally. The next thing I knew she had pushed me down, sat on top of me and began to try and inject me in my arm.

"Stop, stop!" I screamed. This alerted my grandmother and quickly she pulled Janet off me. Janet had this tremendous look of satisfaction on her face as she was sent upstairs.

Whether Janet picked up on my Spiritual energy being different from hers or was she able to discern that any strength I had as a person had been browbeaten out of me. I don't know. Whatever her reasoning, she knew outwardly I was weak and could be overpowered. The result from these experiences has carried over into my adult life. When I go swimming I never put my head under the water and I am terrified of injections.

Another of my father's sisters also owned a public house. Their daughter was six years older than me. They shut the doors as was usual in England, at three pm and opened again at six pm. We were shut out of the house in all weathers for these three hours as they wanted to rest and not be disturbed by kids before they opened up again. When we were let in, my cousin would sometimes have her friends come around.

Each time they came around, they would see how long it would take to get me going, before I lashed out at them. They would take turns to fight me.

With each experience I was learning to get tougher. The more annoyed and angry I became, the more I would hit and kick them.

Of all the young relatives, I was the one that Aunty Ivy asked to be in her wedding party. She came down to our house one day looking so happy.

"Susan," she joyously said, "Will you be my flower girl? I am getting married."

I had never known such excitement as she took me to the shop to buy the dress. It was pastel lemon in layers covered with rosebuds with a headdress that was also covered in rosebuds and had ribbons hanging down the back. The shoes were beautiful white patent leather. I felt I was a real life Angel with a halo. Everybody was extremely happy as the wedding day came and went. The next day was to become the biggest and saddest day of my short life so far. As my Aunty Ivy and her new husband were heading off on their honeymoon my mother said to me cruelly,

"She has gone now and you don't have anywhere to run!"

"Where, where has she gone?" I anxiously asked. "She's coming back?"

I had no concept that now she was married she would be living somewhere else. Aunty Ivy living with my grandmother was all I could and wanted to understand. She was my Aunty Ivy who always took care of me.

When I tried to say how much I would miss her I couldn't and I just cried.

I would still go to my grandmother Florence's house, and Aunty Ivy would come and visit but things were never the same. My grandmother tried one day to let me have fun. My grandfather was asleep on the couch. I found some old makeup left by my Aunty Ivy and I proceeded to make him 'pretty.' I carefully put the blue eye shadow on, followed by a big dollop of rouge and then a very deep red lipstick.

"You will make him angry when he wakes up," my grandmother laughingly said.

"He wants to go down to the pub for a beer and how is he going to do that with all that makeup on his face?"

When he did wake-up and saw his face in the mirror, he mockingly looked in shock. I ran out laughing and laughing. I really loved my grandfather and grandmother.

There were no strong religious beliefs held in my house. We did however live very close to the local St Paul's Church where all our family were christened, as well as many of my aunts and uncles being married there. My brother and I went to Sunday School every week where we would receive Bible stamps to put into our books. The stamps with Jesus on them particularly fascinated me and I would look at them hard and study them. I never used to listen to the Sunday school teachers and what lesson they would be giving connected to these stamps, as Spirit would tell me what Jesus was actually saying. At times it was like I was watching a TV story and it would all be unfolding in front of me.

The church yard became the neighbourhood children's playground as we got older. My brother and I, with the few friends we had, would go out exploring and playing in the church yard. Our favourite game was to run and hide behind the grave stones. At times I would go down there by myself and I would walk around the grave yard touching the headstones. Sitting and talking to the person buried there, I would be told all about their family and what they did, how they died and any messages they had for me. Hearing Spirit was such a part of me now I never questioned or thought about how I was able to do this.

The church doors were never locked. Sneaking inside this day, we opened the large doors and right down the front was a lady playing the organ. I could see her as plain as anything.

I said to the others, "She will tell us off if we start playing in here."

My friends said, "Who will tell us off?"

"The lady playing the organ. Listen to the music."

They said, "There is no lady playing the organ."

"Look. She is looking at us now. She is smiling at us."

It freaked my friends out and they took off running out of that church screaming. I could never understand why those around me could not see or hear what I could.

Finally I made a true friend, Lorraine. Unfortunately she only came to stay during the school holidays with my mother's friend Doris, who lived who lived two doors along from our house. Sometimes I was allowed to stay at their house when she was visiting. Lorraine was my age and when I stayed I slept in her bedroom. One night I heard footsteps coming up the stairs, it was late, and I said to my friend,

"It's all right, they're only ghosts and they are looking for me." I didn't know how else to describe them at my age.

"They are looking for me because I am not in my house, I am not in my bed."

Lorraine became hysterical. She ran out screaming telling her aunty Doris what I had said. I didn't mean to frighten her, as they never scare me. That was the end of sleeping over at Lorraine's house when she visited.

I would try and tell Lorraine and the other children about what I was seeing and hearing, but this only frightened them more. I could not understand why other people could not see what I was seeing and hearing. My mother had obviously seen Spirit somewhere in her life but had not believed what she was seeing. I remember this Sunday night, my father wasn't home and my mother went to bed at about 9pm. For some silly reason I had this idea of scaring my mother. I put a sheet over myself and I crept down the stairs. There was a light coming from under the bedroom door and I waited until she put her light out and then went in. I stood next to her bed going "whoooooooo," and touched her face. She sprung out of bed, grabbed the sheet, seeing it was me she smacked me around the head and sent me off to bed.

Sue aged 5 years with the bike she used to transport the local cats and dogs on, Birmingham, 1959.

Moving House

It had been a long time coming for the local Council to recognise that people could no longer live in the squalid conditions that we endured nestled in amongst the factories. The block of twelve houses where I had lived for the first eight years of my life was going to be knocked down and another factory was to be built in their place.

At this time in England when you were going to be relocated from one Council house to another, they gave you options on three houses or flats to look at. If you didn't take one of those three, you would be put anywhere they found and there would be no choice. The letter eventually came from the Council advising us that there were two properties that we could go and look at.

My father, my brother and I went to see the first two flats but we didn't like them. My mother had set her heart on a separate house with a garden. Everybody was tense in the house as we knew there was only one more chance of selecting a house that we wanted to move to. In time, the third letter came advising us that they would send the keys through. It was in an area where some of my aunts and uncles lived and there was great excitement and anticipation that this could be the house.

It was Saturday afternoon as Dad, I and my brother set off to look at this new house and Mum stayed at home with my sister. When we finally arrived after catching two buses and then a long walk I could not believe what I was seeing. Spirit told me as soon as I saw the house with the huge garden that this was going to be where I would live for a very long time. We opened the door of the house and went in. We all gasped as it was so much bigger than our house. The kitchen even contained a sink with hot running water and there was a bathroom with its own bath. The toilet was outside but it was going to be our own toilet. My own toilet! I remember looking at it and thinking what it was going to be like not having to hold on for so long before running across the yard to go to the toilet.

We all went our different ways in the house. I ran upstairs and went into one of the bedrooms. There was a coldness in there, a coldness I was learning to recognise as that of someone who has passed over but decides to linger on this earth plane. I felt it was an old man who had lived here. I also sensed a woman but I didn't share any of this with the others. Outside, the huge garden was surrounded by a fence and the tall grass was uncut. There were two enormous pine trees in the overgrown front garden and there was farmland surrounding the back of the property. It was like a scene from Alice in Wonderland. I began to imagine the adventures I could have.

We took the two buses again and eventually arrived home. Mum was bathing my sister in the bowl on the dining table.

"Well then," my mother said, with a pleading look on her face.

"It was horrible. The grass is taller than me and there are snakes in the garden," I said trying not to give it all away.

"No we can't have it. It's not for us," Dad chimed in.

My mother was visibly upset. She had a fearful look on her face.

"What is going to become of us?" She began to cry.

We all began to realise how mean we were being and the joke had to end.

"We are going to have it," my father said with the biggest smirk on his face.

Finally there was elation on my mother's face and this was the first time I ever saw my mother hug my father.

Even though the conditions of our old house were dreadful, it was still hard leaving. This was all I knew and I was afraid of the changes that would be ahead of me. A number of families had already moved and it was like they had disappeared into thin air as nobody knew where they had gone to. The biggest ache in my heart was for my grandmother Florence. They were not coming with us and, as yet, they had not found a new house to move to. I knew I would never be able to run to her house again and find the comfort that I needed so often. I began to have dreams of seeing my grandmother having to move to these old derelict houses and she would say to me,

"I can't leave this house as this is all I know."

My grandparents were eventually relocated to an estate a long way away. We did not have a car so visiting always involved very long bus rides. On Saturdays we three children would visit my grandparents, but she was never the same as she didn't know her neighbours and all her friends had moved to other areas. She was very, very lonely. At Christmas my grandfather couldn't endure these long hours involved to get to our new house and so we only celebrated with my grandmother.

The experiences with Spirit increased and the energies became very strong with the moving to the new house. I was eight years old. The main Spirit energies were a man and a woman. Sometimes they would appear and I could see them. We hadn't been long in the house, it was a Saturday night. My father was out and my mother, brother and sister were down stairs. I was in the bedroom, as I used to go to my bedroom to get away from the others. I heard someone come up the stairs and along the landing. We had this very old door handle and it was a latch that you pushed across, so I quickly locked the door. Sometimes it would stick and you couldn't get it open. I knew there was someone out there and I got this feeling of an energy that wasn't friendly. I jumped as a loud banging began on the door. I wanted to believe it was my brother playing a joke on me but I was still very scared. I waited for a couple of hours until I thought there was no one there. Quietly I went downstairs and complained about my brother to my mother.

"He's been banging on my door and playing jokes on me. He's been upstairs scaring me."

She shouted as she said my brother had been downstairs all night with her and hadn't moved from the fire. I knew there was someone trying to get in to my room and I was told it was the Spirit of the old man who used to live in the house and he did not like our presence in his house. We were intruders as far as he was concerned.

Some things do not change with a move to a new location. Dad continued to go out drinking with his brothers on the weekends, we were still extremely poor and my mother remained depressed and continued to speak angrily to me at every opportunity. With the help of all those on the other side and the resolve and strength that I had obviously been born with I began to develop a real fighting strength within me. My mother had great difficulty with this and with no control over any of her husband's ways, tried to enforce on me complete control of all that I did. She continually wanted to break me down. I had no cellar or grandmothers to escape to - instead I retreated to an old deck chair outside in the back garden. I would cuddle myself up in a blanket covering my head, a bit like a miniature tent that only I could fit into.

Very quickly I would drift off and enter a deep meditative-like state. Spirit would then place this big leather bound book, which seemed huge, in front of me. The leather looked worn, the pages were very thin and they were being turned at a speed that was humanly impossible. My eyes would scan the pages and I could hear Spirit's voices whispering, whispering so quickly the utterings were unrecognisable to my ear. With the monotonous sound of the whisperings and the peace I was finding, the hours would fly by. I spent many peaceful days sitting here outside, right through my childhood and up until the age of twenty three, the age I was married and I left home. I still do this now even if it's cold and wet as it is my way of escaping and catching up with myself. It is a wonderful way of connecting and learning from Spirit for me.

Unbeknown to me at the time, it was the Arkashic Records and the Books of Wisdom that Spirit was showing to me. It was pages and pages of old records of my life times and old records of knowledge and wisdom. Spirit had begun teaching me the old ways of many things. The Other Side was providing my tuition in life and all things Spiritual. I can now at any time ask a question of the Universe, and it is answered. I speak only the truth from what Spirit tells me and they continue to be the only teachers I have ever had. When I saw the Secret DVD recently I thought, I know that book, I know what they are talking about as it was knowledge that I had learnt as a young child.

* * * *

Life was easier at the new house for my mother and for all of us. I am sure we were now cleaner with our own bath and having our own toilet was a luxury. I no longer had to sleep in an attic with my brother as I now shared a bedroom and a bed with my sister where she would line all her dolls up in the bed and I would be hanging out the side. Wetting the bed was something I had grown out of but unfortunately my sister hadn't. I was the one that was always blamed and scolded for the wet bed and was made to clean it up even though I tried to protest my innocence. Finally we had separate beds. Monday continued to be wash day, but now with a twist. We did have a washing machine, a twin tub, at the new house, but my mother didn't understand how it worked. The clothes still had to be soaked in the bath on a Sunday night, stopping any of us having a bath before the school week began.

The tremendous headaches that had started at the old house began to get worse at the new house. I would try to tell my mother about the headaches, but she would not listen and I received no sympathy. This one particularly bad Sunday morning, my mother was at the sink and I told her how I didn't feel very well. The next minute I had blacked out on the kitchen floor. When I came to I had my head in the dog's bowl. She never moved from the sink. She kept on peeling the potatoes. It was the treatment I was trying hard to learn to accept.

I started to think that maybe I had cancer. Oh, how my life would become different if this was the case. Maybe my parents might begin to love me and look after me. Would I be better dead, then began to cross my mind. When I was so low, Spirit would come to me as I lay in bed at night and they would repeat the words that I had heard so often on my small red plastic telephone at my old house.

"You are a special little girl. You have a special job to do. We are here to look after you. You are never alone."

"If I'm not to die, can you put me in another house, please? I'm not meant to be here. Please take me away from here you have put me in the wrong place," I would pleadingly ask Spirit.

I was never taken to the doctors and it was never discovered why I was getting these headaches. Were they caused through the stress of living in this family? With the lack of concern being shown I decided then this was not my real family. Maybe Mum and Dad weren't my real parents.

Every day, I began saying to myself,

"I don't belong to this family, how could they treat me this badly, I must be adopted!"

I began madly searching the house for my adoption papers every time my parents went out. This was the only explanation I could find as to why my mother continued to be angry with me and why my father stayed away from me.

Eventually I did find my birth certificate and I did belong to them. So why would they treat me like this? Why would they say it was black if I said it was white? I can now see that I chose to be put into that family to learn about negativity and to find ways of seeing the positive and learning that there is always light in all situations. If it hadn't been for my connection with Spirit I know I wouldn't be here now.

This led me to believe that I was not wanted and that I was somehow different from other children. I still wanted to have friends to play with and adults to like me and often I would draw pictures of myself surrounded by adults, and the adults would be saying,

"Susan's a lovely girl and we would like you to come to our house."

Spirit must have heard me pleading to go to other people's houses and organised it so I was regularly given time out from my family.

In the back garden of the new house. In the foreground from left to right Sue's mother Violet with a cousin, Sue and sister Carol, 1964.

During the long seven week summer holiday, I was often sent to stay with different relatives. My brother and sister always stayed home during these holidays.

One holiday when I was 10, I went to stay with my cousin Linda, who was three years older than me and an only child. They took me on holiday and we went to Margate for two weeks. We had such a wonderful holiday and I didn't want to go home. As we pulled up to my house, I was crying.

"Don't you want to see your Mum and Dad?" my Aunty curiously asked me.

"No," I meekly said, "I want to stay on holiday with you." I knew what it would be like living again with my mother.

My aunty took my hand and walked me up the path to the house.

"Hello Barbara," my Mother greeted us as she opened the front door smiling.

"Have you had a lovely time, Susan?" Aunty Barbara asked me.

I was petrified to answer her. I knew my mother's smile wasn't genuine, but my aunty didn't. I had seen my mother put the face on often before to give the impression that everything is fine.

Before I could answer, my aunty proceeded to tell my mother what a good girl I had been and I had been no trouble.

"You have had a nice time, haven't you Susan?" my aunty again said.

"Yes thank you very much," I replied thinking, what's going to happen now!

My mother said goodbye and then shut the door. She turned to me, I will never forget it, and said,

"Right, you are home now. You are in the real world so take that smile off your face."

I ran up the stairs and cried and cried.

Years later Linda shared with me how jealous she was of me when I came to stay. She mistakenly thought my Aunty Barbara loved me more than her as it was always,

"Susan this and Susan that." When I shared with her family after my mother passed over, how I had been treated in my childhood, my cousin understood. My auntie's suspicions about the state of my family life were confirmed.

Sue aged 8 years old.

Life Lessons Increase

When we moved to the new house I started at a new school in the middle term. It was the loneliest time of my whole life. I had no friends and couldn't seem to make any. It was compounded because I couldn't read or write properly. I compensated for the lack of reading and writing ability by developing a very strong memory. The school must have been concerned about me as the teacher asked my parents to come to see her on parent/teacher night. My parents had never ever come to school before.

"You better have not told anyone anything," my mother fearfully said.

What was it that I was supposed to have not told anybody?

"I haven't, I haven't told anyone anything."

The teachers told them how withdrawn I was and how I didn't interact with the other children. My parents when they came home told me how annoyed and embarrassed they were by me and they only seemed concerned about what the teacher thought of them. I was offered no extra help to improve my school work and it has only been through hard work in my years after school that I have now learnt to read and write to a high standard.

My mother's dislike of me seemed to intensify when my father wasn't there. If I went to sit next to her she would tell me to go away.

"You make me feel sick," she would say.

There were no hugs, or cuddles or good nights, no stories to enjoy. I did not know any other way. I thought this was normal.

"Susan," she called to me one day when I was sitting by myself next to the open coal fire in the living room. My mother called my brother over as well. She brought the newspaper out.

"Read this line here," she asked me.

I couldn't make out the words, let alone pronounce them.

"Tell her she's stupid; tell her she's stupid and thick," she said to my brother.

He dutifully did so, with great gusto.

I found out later, it was her frustration with her own inability to read and write and she was bullying me to make herself feel better.

One night when Mum was out cleaning I decided to tell my father how my mother treated me. I spoke of the nasty things she would say to me and how I had headaches and she wouldn't listen. Well Dad told Mum what I had said and of course she denied it and said it is all in my head and that I tell lies. He smacked me for telling lies and told me not to tell lies about my mother. I now knew I had no support and went further into my shell.

My younger sister was the world to my parents. I never heard my sister receive nasty comments from my mother. My father spent time with her and would play games with her when home. I would sit and watch and sometimes get the confidence to ask to join in.

"Please, can I have a ride on your back, now?" I begged my father as my sister was having her turn.

My mother quickly turned to me and said,

"Get away from him!"

I could not understand why there was to be no contact with my father.

From that time on I became very despondent with feelings of hopelessness. At the age of 10 I decided not to be here any more. I went to my brother's room upstairs and climbed out onto the window ledge. I could see myself falling down onto the concrete below. This was the only way. How desperate I had become.

Mrs Bevan, the next door neighbour, who was so kind to us, was hanging out the washing. She looked up and shouted to my mother,

"Violet, Susan is climbing out of the window."

My mother came running up the stairs.

"Get in here! You are embarrassing me."

"I don't want to live in this house anymore. I want to go!"

"Don't be silly, you can't kill yourself," I heard Spirit tell me.

"No I will not stop, you are so mean to me," I cried to my mother.

She put her arm out and grabbed me and pulled me back in through the window.

"You know what from now on your life will be hell," was her sadistic reply.

If it had been bad before, it was certainly going to be worse now.

My mother found a new job from four thirty to nine at night cleaning in the local area. I would come home from school just before she left and each night I would heat up and serve Dad his dinner that mum had prepared that day. There was never any dinner made for us. As he ate I would stand behind him silently pleading for him to leave a potato or some gravy that I could eat. Then when he left the table I would get a bit of bread and wipe the plate with it to get some taste of the meal. My mother had a thing about food and Spirit has told me it came from the war times with rations. Tins in the cupboard had rust on them, but we often went hungry. We did have dinner at the weekends but I can not remember having dinner during the week until I started work at seventeen.

On Sundays when we would sometimes have the relatives over for afternoon tea Mum would bake the most wonderful assortment of cakes and biscuits. All that was left over was put away for my father to have in his lunches that week. What joy it was when I had the courage to open a tin and steal a treat without being found out. My mother would put on the pretence and put on a big show on these Sundays to the relatives making out that we were a normal family. However when they left she would negatively talk about them. She actually didn't want them there at all. As a family we never received an invitation to visit them at their houses.

My brother had obviously seen how efficient I was at making and serving tea on these Sunday nights with my mother out and my father still at work until six o'clock, my brother would make me his servant and I would have to serve him.

"Make me a cup of tea, Servant" he would say as he sat in the chair waiting. I finally got the courage to stand up to him. I went into the kitchen and found this new stainless steel teapot.

"Do you really want a cup of tea?" I shouted out.

"Yes," he said.

So out of the kitchen I stormed and I hit him as hard as I could over the head with the teapot. As soon as mum came home, I was in trouble. He told her in the most fabricated way of what I had done, but never told her about the way he ordered me around. She would not listen to my side of the story and I was severely punished.

Spirit assisted me to develop a way of escaping from the world I was living in. I was taught how to leave my body as it was sleeping. It is like being awake whilst you are dreaming and I now know it is called Astral Travel. Going to bed at night became exciting as this new ability intensified. To ensure I travelled at will, I would clear my mind of all my other thoughts and emotions. We had only just moved into the new house and one night after falling asleep I found myself out of bed, hovering high above and looking down on myself. I began to perfect this ability and after a while with a lot of practice I was able to go to different places. I found I could travel on purpose to people in their own homes.

Helen Sweetman, who was an only child, lived across the road with her parents and grandmother and she became a good friend. They had a little black poodle, which slept in the kitchen. Her father, who worked different shifts at British Leyland, would take us to school in his white car on his days off. On the other days I would walk over to her house in the morning to meet her so we could walk to school. Standing on the step outside one morning I got to thinking about what her house was like inside as I had never been invited in. Often I would tell Helen about what I could hear, see and do but it was always too unbelievable for her and she thought I was making it all up. It was time, I decided to prove to Helen that I did see dead people and that there were things I could do. I planned to visit her house that night, and tell her the next day about what I had seen.

That night, I excitedly went upstairs, went to bed and to sleep. The next minute I could see myself in my pyjamas going across the street and I walked straight through the door into the living room. The dog came through from the kitchen and began barking at me as he could see me.

"Shoosh Peppy," I telepathically said, "Be quiet."

The outside street light lit up the house inside. I went up the stairs and I went into the first room on the left. It was Helen's room and I could see all her things on her bed. Helen wasn't in the bed. I went to the next room on the landing. Helen was in bed with her mother. The night lamp on the table was on and I took note of everything so I could tell her. To me it was like a game. I then went into her grandmother's room, took note of the nightgown she had on, and then came down the stairs. Instantly I was back in bed.

The next day I woke up, got ready and then went over the road to collect Helen for school. When she came out I told her excitedly,

"I've got something to tell you. Last night after I went to bed and to sleep I travelled over to your house. I can tell you exactly what you were wearing, and you weren't in your bed in your room, and your Dad wasn't there."

Unbeknown to me, he had to cover the night shift. I described everything in her bedroom; I described her grandmother's old fashioned cotton nightie with the frill up around her neck. She laughed and called me freaky.

I did it again the next night, but this time it scared me. I walked through the doorway and into the lounge where there was a large grandfather clock on the wall. When her grandfather passed away, it stopped. It couldn't be repaired, even though they tried. The dog began to bark at me again and then I looked over and there was a man in Spirit. He looked at me and said

"I am Helen's grandfather. What are you doing?"

"Can you see me?" I asked.

"You can see me can't you? Tell them I am back now and the clock will start."

Well I went out of that house very quickly and went back home.

The next day on the way to school I asked Helen if her clock had started in the lounge.

Helen looked at me in wonderment, "We came down stairs this morning and it was going. We heard the large ticking."

"Your grandfather was here last night and he said to tell you he's back and the clock will start." I described him and it was him.

I realised that if Spirit can see me and I can see them that it is a two way thing. This was getting thrilling.

I now truly believed I could fly out of my body. I moved on to think that if I could fly in my sleep I could fly in the daytime, so I started to practice. I believed I had wings. Outside in the school playground was a dip, down to the tennis courts which had a wire netting fence around it. Every day I would go outside to the courts, take a run down it and start flapping my arms hoping to take off. Bang, I was on the ground. I used to get crowds around me. Further and further back I would go to get my speed up. They all thought I was insane. The gym teacher came out and told me how ridiculous I was and I had to stop because I was bending the fence. You could see the shape of my body imprinted on it. This definitely didn't help me in the friendship stakes.

At night I would lie on my bed, which faced the door of my bedroom, watching the passed over people coming up the stairs. They would sit on my bed and talk to me until I went to sleep. I could see them as plain as day, as they appeared solid. Many were my passed over relatives as I had seen them in photographs. They always seemed to be there for me especially when I was really down and at times they seemed so close it was as if they were trying to hug me. As I have developed I now see them as mist. When I was young if a mist had come and sat on my bed I wouldn't have understood who or what they were. I needed them to be solid.

At first I thought they were ordinary people but when they had finished talking to me they would get up and walk straight through the wall. When I went to school I used to ask the other children if they have people that come and see you at night time and sit on your bed and talk to you. They would say, "Your mother and father?"

I would say, "No, because they walk through the wall."

This again added to the idea that I was crazy. I must have possessed great faith in Spirit during these days as I am sure other children would have given up with no support or assurance from the adults around them.

As I grew older I wanted to start to experiment more with some of the ability that I had and I wanted to know more about what was on the other side. I knew there were things beyond this earth plane that we couldn't explain. I was in class one day and I made up all the letters of the alphabet, put them in a circle and got a glass.

"Who wants to do this with me?" I asked. I had seen this thing called Ouija Board on Television and it had intrigued me.

Spirit had warned me,

"This is not a good idea; you do not know what you are playing with!"

I went on with the 'game' regardless. Seven others in the class were keen to join in and so we each put one finger on the glass. It started going berserk and moving extremely quickly around the table. Some took their fingers off, petrified. The windows on a catch opened out for no reason. Some of the others began screaming. Even though I knew nothing of the dark side it didn't scare me. I thought it was funny to invoke Spirit in this way. Then I started receiving thoughts in my head about each one and I started giving messages to each of them. I told one girl that her grandmother was very ill, which was true. This game did not have the desired effect of making friends, in fact it was just the opposite. The Ouija Board had added to the idea that I was obviously weird and different and people started to stay away from me.

I began to be a target for practical jokes from my classmates. One early evening as my father lay in bed with a sore back I was summoned to his bedroom. Before I could even say a word he began to yell at me and tell me how filthy and disgusting I was. My mother had found a dirty joke written on a piece of paper in my school bag. I had never seen it before and obviously someone had placed it in my bag as a joke. My father had always been a very strict disciplinarian and he ruled the house with an iron rod when he was home. He had very strong ideas about mixing with the opposite sex and what one might get up to. I was just thirteen and I knew that I must never speak to or even look at boys.

One day Helen Sweetman and I were walking home from school and it began raining and so we sheltered in the woods nearby. Two boys from school happened to be there as well and we just began talking to them. As it was getting late my father had come out looking for me. He happened to see Helen and me talking to these two boys and unfortunately I didn't see him. By the time I arrived home my mother was waiting for me. I walked around to the back door.

"Where have you been?" my mother accusingly asked me.

I tried to explain to her about the rain and sheltering in the woods.

"You are in big trouble your father has gone looking for you and has seen you with boys!" she began shouting.

I went into the bathroom to dry myself and the next thing I knew dad was standing there. As he asked me where I had been for so long after school he began taking off his large leather belt.

I tried to explain,

"I was walking home with Helen and we stopped in the woods when it began to rain."

"You have been with boys," he said with such a maddening look on his face.

"I spoke to them," I timidly replied.

"You are a liar, you have been with boys." Out came his big leather belt and with much strength he repeatedly hit me across my back. I was screaming and pleaded with him to stop. Because I had answered him back he said I would get more.

It must have been bad because finally my mother stood up for me and said,

"That's enough." I was crying.

All she could say to me was,

"You have really upset your father."

I looked at her and said,

"Upset! Have you seen what he has done to me?"

For months after that neither spoke to me. I didn't exist. It was isolation and mental torture.

During the week that my grandmother died I hadn't been to see her as I was involved with a production at school. She had fallen over on the ice and injured her knee and being unable to move she became sick, caught a chest infection and died of pneumonia. They discovered at this time that she was also diabetic, which explained why she drank so much water. Even though she and my granddad lived some distance away, every Monday after school I had hopped on the bus and gone to see her. I would put her hair in rollers and do her hair, then sit and chat with her. We really did have a special bond.

I will never forget the day the policeman came to the door and told my mother that her mother had died. Guilt set in with me that I hadn't been to see her and hadn't helped her that week. I sobbed uncontrollably as I thought of her. She was so gentle and kind. My grandmother died when I was fourteen and I wasn't allowed to go to the funeral.

"Children don't go to funerals," my mother coldly told me.

My heart ached as I wanted to see her one more time. My grandmother had been the one special person in my life who had always been there for me. I do see her often now though in Spirit.

After she passed my mother got even angrier. Every Saturday afternoon after she had been to the salon, which was her treat, she would have to go to my grandfather's and do all the housework. I used to fear my mother coming home as she would always be in a foul mood. My father would be in the bath getting ready to go out without her and here she was with her hair done and not being taken out on a Saturday night.

Work Experience

I began working at the hair dressing salon when I was twelve years old. I worked there for four years and my pay was one pound for the thirteen hours I worked each week. Millie was the owner of the Salon and she was very, very strict and extremely old fashioned. The salon was above a haberdashery shop. I used to sweep up and wash hair and sometimes I was allowed to practice on the model out the back. My hair was cut very short and each time I wanted a cut I had to pay for it myself. When Millie wasn't there, I would ask the seniors,

"Can I have a trim or a cut?"

When Millie returned she would say,

"Are you sure you haven't had a haircut?"

"No Millie," was my meek reply.

"You better not have. You know you would have to put the money in the till if you did."

At school I was still having difficulty, so it was often discussed as to what I could do when I left school. My mother used to have her hair done at the salon every Saturday afternoon. Millie the owner approached my mother saying,

"I need to talk to you about Susan and the possibility of her taking on an apprenticeship here. She has very good skills and I want to send her on a part-time, five year course to a private beautician school."

My mother thought it was a wonderful opportunity and spoke to me about it. I was against going. Not only did I not like Millie as she was very controlling, but after the five years I would be bonded to her.

"You do it and then you leave," my mother said, trying to pressurise me into taking the job. I couldn't be dishonest with Millie.

My mother was annoyed with me but I stood my ground. Underneath I knew there was something else I was supposed to do with my life. I did enjoy hairdressing and I would have loved to have taken it on as a career but if I had of I would not be doing what I am doing now.

When I chose to be born into this family, I must have known that my mother would develop skills in me of assisting others without expecting anything in return. I would be always doing errands for my mother and I grew to love being around older people. They always seem to have so much knowledge, and I have always enjoyed talking to them and listening to their memories and what they have to say. I had heard about this elderly man through Millie at the hairdressers. I volunteered to go and visit him every day to do any little jobs that he might need doing. So I wouldn't disturb him he gave me a key to the house. He was very quiet and said very little and as a fourteen year old I thought this was very rude. He would write a list of the jobs he wanted me to do and that could be the shopping, cleaning the house, or doing the washing up.

"Hello Mr M. how are you today?" I said as I walked in this day. He was sitting on the couch. There was no response from him as usual and I thought he must have been cold as he looked a bit pale and still had his coat and hat on.

I tidied around and washed up even though there was nothing written on the list for me to do. So I did my bit and said goodbye as I shut the door and went home. I didn't go the next day because I had something on at school and it was two days before I went back. I was having trouble getting the key into the lock when the next door neighbour came out and said,

"You won't get in there. He died!"

"He what?" I said in disbelief.

He had been sitting there dead when I was cleaning around him. I said to the woman,

"I wondered why he didn't answer me when I spoke to him." I had never seen a dead person, even though I talked to those that had passed over all the time. In his Will he left me these four, small Ming vases. I took them home and showed them to my Dad and he said,

"They are worth something." I never saw them again after that. They were real antiques and my father had sold them.

Ouija boards came into my life again when I was working at the hairdressers. A new senior started and one day when we were talking about Spirit she told me she had a board. I had learned not to tell people I knew things or that I spoke to Spirit. She invited me to go around to her house as her parents were away and we could play with the board. The trainee junior and I went around. We got the board out and we started to work with it. The senior unbeknown to me spoke French. As the letters were coming through I couldn't understand them. The senior realised the first name was in French and it was a male. He had been hung for crimes committed. We were sitting there when we heard noises upstairs, just like feet walking around. I said to the senior,

"Is someone home?"

"No," she said, "there are only us three here."

"Well, you have got someone upstairs in your room walking around." It was him, the Frenchman walking around upstairs. It was a negative energy and he felt nasty.

Feeling very uneasy I said, "Look at the time, I have to go home."

The other girl came as well. We left the senior in the house all by herself and she had to sleep downstairs all night as he wouldn't go.

My brother also began dabbling with the other side. He had a proper board but we weren't to tell Dad. He decided to hide it in the shed in the garden where Dad used to spend time, doing goodness knows what. My father had this eye infection, which was getting worse and wouldn't come right even with eye drops. I said to my brother,

"I know what it is; it's the evil off that board in the shed. You will have to tell our Dad."

"No," he said ,"He will go mad."

Alan did tell him and my father went mad and got him to show him where it was. My father wanted to burn it but my brother was to return it to the person he borrowed it from. After that his eye started to get better and the operation that was planned to fix the eye did not happen. When my brother bought an old car and kept the board in the boot, it caught fire. No one knew why but I believe it was that board.

When you play with Ouija Boards and open the door to the other side you will get people good and bad coming through. That's why you need a prayer at the beginning and asking for white light or Archangel Michael for protection and only bring through positive energies. I didn't know this at the time and do not recommend playing with Ouija Boards.

As I became older, my dream state started to become very powerful and provided answers for me about my life. They were extremely vivid and very real at the time. One unforgettable dream when I was fourteen continued for a number of nights and is still with me today. It was a foggy night, in my dream as I walked down the path and through the back gate out of our property. I was taking our corgi dog for a walk. Within a few seconds, I could feel someone behind me. I kept asking,

"Who is this?'

I sensed it was male and I just knew he was going to hurt me. The first night of my dream he came up behind me with a rope and pulled the rope tight and that was it. The next day the dream was still with me. It was very strong.

The next night I began the dream again, down the path with the dog, open the gate, he was there again. I wasn't able to turn around to see him. He had a gun and he shot me.

On the third night I knew I had to turn around to look at him. This night I felt a knife go right into the base of my spine and start to cut through. The pain was incredible. I turned around to look at him. He was dressed in a coat and hat. I talked to him telepathically and asked why he was doing this to me. He just stared at me. I fell to my knees and that was the end of me.

The next day in real life, I ran into my mother's room to look at my back in the mirror. There was this massive scar on my lower back and you could see where stitches had been put in. I went and showed my mother. Of course she didn't believe me and insisted I had scratched myself. This did not stop me going to school and showing everyone. The following night in my continuing dream I saw all my family and relations standing around a coffin. When I came up they parted and when I looked into the coffin I saw myself in that coffin. I believe now it was a past life that I was living through again.

When I look back at this dream I feel that this was the end of that part of my life. It was a death and a rebirth as my abilities started to increase again. That scar has been checked by two surgeons. When I was at my first job I slipped on the ice and hurt my back. I went to the doctors and he sent me onto the orthopaedic hospital as I couldn't move one of my legs. As soon as I went into the cubicle I knew he was going to look at my back and ask me where this scar had come from. When he saw it he said,

"Oh, I can see you have already had a back operation. This is definitely an operation site."

"You wouldn't believe me if I told you," I said and so he never said anything. Years on I slipped over again and rehurt my back. This next surgeon also commented on my previous 'operation' and said whoever had done it had done a very neat and tidy job.

Again I told the surgeon, "I haven't had an operation."

"Well," he said, "for insurance purposes I have to write this down and so I am going to sit here until you tell me, otherwise I can't write out the insurance."

This was the first time I told someone who wasn't a believer. He was absolutely shocked and amazed. He said, "I can't say anything else. Who ever has done it," he said, "they have done a really good job." Spirit had obviously sewn me up really well.

Having made the decision not to be a hairdresser, I stayed on at school for an extra year, as I was petrified of going to work. Difficulty with reading and writing was still plaguing me and I continued to rely on remembering everything. I began learning typing and shorthand as this was seen as a way of opening up a job opportunity for me. My childhood dream of working in an office could actually be a reality.

Eventually the time came to leave school. I found employment as an office junior in an architect's office. It was extremely difficult as I still couldn't spell properly and I had to do dictaphone typing. Making it up became the order of the day, as I couldn't understand what they were talking about. Obviously typing was not my forte. When it was realised I was having extreme difficulty, the typing was given to somebody else and I was given the job of filing and taking the plans down to the town hall to register them, doing the banking as well as making the tea.

Even though I was working, I was still shown no respect and was over disciplined by my parents. My job every Wednesday was to do the ironing which entailed everything being ironed from underwear, towels, flannels, sheets and every family member's clothes. This Wednesday I had arranged to go out and so I hurriedly did all the ironing and was preparing to leave when I was told I was going nowhere. It was more than I could take. I went upstairs, packed my things, wrote a departure letter and walked out the door to stay at my friend's house. Unfortunately my father threatened me with being a 'ward of the court' and so home I had to go. From here on in I only slept at home as I was no longer regarded as part of the family and they did not attempt to make any contact with me.

When I began work, I also began drinking alcohol excessively as I discovered that alcohol numbed my pain. One night when I was really drunk I let my mother have it. Everything that had been stored up all these years came out. She was disgusted and enraged with what was coming out of my mouth. The next thing I vomited all over the carpet in the bedroom. This began the next long withdrawal of communication between my parents and me, as again I was cut off and nobody spoke to me. The drinking went to new heights and I began drinking anything and everything - usually straight.

I was finally shocked into giving up alcohol when the surgeon who had removed my wisdom teeth asked me if I drank a lot of alcohol. My liver was enlarged and if I didn't do something about it now, I would not be living long, this scared me and I cut right back. Over the years I have become allergic to alcohol. As you start to work with Spirit your vibration gets higher and alcohol and certain foods cause reactions. When people come to me, I can tell if they are taking drugs as they have like little black pinholes in their auras.

My First Boyfriend

Spirit can speak to us with guidance but if we do not want to listen, their messages will fall on deaf ears and we will embark on a journey of intense learning. I was to discover this truth in the most horrible of ways. I had just begun work at the architect's office and my childhood friend Helen Sweetman, contacted me to go out on the town. It had to be done in secret as my parents still had not relented on their rules regarding me and boys and my father still controlled me to the limit. When I first met Roy there was just something about him that I was instantly attracted to, he became my first boyfriend when I was seventeen and he was nineteen.

"Stay away from him. He is not good for you."

I heard Spirit telling me once again but I did not want to listen as I was hell bent on going out with this guy. When you grow up in a home, where every thought and action is controlled, you learn no other way. I had stepped into a relationship that perfectly mirrored my home life. I thought his controlling nature was normal. The warning signals, besides those of Spirit, were all there in front of me. I did notice how badly he treated his mother and how aggressive he was. If I said the wrong thing he would put me down and embarrass me in front of others telling me I was stupid. I wasn't allowed to look at anyone else or allowed to speak to anyone else. His possessiveness of me, I thought was because he really loved me. In some bizarre way I was helpless to move from this relationship.

Roy had a sad episode in his life. At the age of fifteen, and the youngest of four, he found his father having a heart attack and he tried to revive him, but couldn't. He carried a lot of guilt that he had let his father die. Counselling was never carried out, and now Roy saw nothing wrong in this behaviour. Often he was high on the drugs he used to take and being naive in these days, I didn't realise. Spirit eventually told me what he was up to and warned me to stay away from taking anything he offered me.

I had been going out with him for two years and his abuse was worsening. I had black eyes, I would say I slipped over, he would hit me in places on my body, that no-one could see. He kicked me, pushed me down stairs, tried to put my head through a television. I became terrified of him, but could not leave him.

"Do you want a sandwich?" he asked one day when I was visiting.

"Yes," I replied, thinking that finally he was being nice to me.

"Well you can make it and make mine as well." I started to make the sandwich and he said something and I didn't hear what he said. He picked up a knife and he held it against my throat.

"When you talk to me you talk to me properly. I could slit your throat and wouldn't think twice about it."

Even his friends seemed to be under his spell. One of his friends had been travelling home on the same bus as me and saw me talk to a guy who I used to go to school with. It was completely innocent. Roy confronted me, outside work when I was walking to the bus stop the next day.

"Who was the person you have been talking to on the bus?"

I meekly replied, "I went to school with him."

Roy grabbed my beautiful black woollen coat that I was wearing. It had big coloured buttons and I had saved so hard to buy it. He grabbed me with so much force that all the buttons were ripped off the coat and they scattered over the footpath and gutter. I was crying as I scrambled to pick up my buttons from the ground.

Roy knew that my job in the architect's office was to handle the petty cash. He would often ask me about it; how much was there, where it was kept, was it locked up. In my naiveté I thought little of his many questions. One morning I arrived at work at eight thirty and there were police cars outside. The drawer where the petty cash tin was held had been smashed opened and the tin was gone. The police questioned me, and took fingerprints from the desk and left.

Roy rang me unexpectedly in the morning and asked, "What are you doing for lunch?"

I was so excited that we were going out to lunch together and the morning couldn't go fast enough. When we met he took me to a shoe shop and bought me a new pair of shoes. Over lunch, he said to me,

"Those shoes were brought with money from out of

your petty cashbox!"

He knew he had too much control over me for me to tell management at work what he had done. They never did find out who stole the money, and I never wore those shoes. After this I no longer wanted to work there and began looking for another job. I was under Roy's spell and I knew no way of how I was going to break-up with him. My self-esteem was low and my self respect was gone.

"He is going to hurt you more, you have to leave him before you have nothing left. He is seeing other girls and you do have a choice in all of this."

I began listening to Spirit and I started to think about leaving him. I tried a number of times but he would come around and I was like putty in his hands again. He proposed to me and we became engaged. Everything would change now I stupidly thought.

"You will never marry him," my mother said.

"Yes I will," I answered her back, "I know you don't like him."

"He's cheating on you. I know he is," my mother sneeringly told me.

I will never know if my mother was just saying this or if she did know. Anyway I just didn't want to know and why would I listen to my mother? Her telling me this just made me more determined to continue going out with him.

It did, however start to play on my mind. I was lying in bed one night after having been out with him and Spirit began talking to me and telling me how he was operating.

"You go out with him, he tells you he has to get up early for work, you come home on the bus and then he goes around the corner and meets another woman."

This proved too much for me and I knew I had to do something about it. I was listening to Spirit, this time and I decided I was going to check up on him by astral travelling and see if he was doing what I was hearing from Spirit. I checked the time as I went out, something I always did and went to his room. He wasn't there. He had an old fashioned oak wardrobe and I was guided to look above this. Above his wardrobe were what appeared to be letters. I travelled home and the next morning, I was distraught when I awoke, as I realised what I had discovered and that Spirit and my mother were telling the truth.

A couple of days later I went to his house knowing he would not be there.

"He is not home," his mother said as she answered the door.

"Okay, but can I go to the bathroom?" I knew the bathroom was upstairs. Quickly I got into his room, pulled the chair over to the wardrobe, stretched up and got the letters. They were from this girl that he had been seeing and he had asked her to marry him. We had been going out for four years and we were going to get married.

Feelings of disbelief and betrayal overwhelmed me. What was I going to do? How could I get back at him? Anger and revenge were all I knew and somehow I was going to teach him a lesson.

I returned another night when I knew he was out and

his mother was on her way out to Bingo. I was very calculating and began preparing for this. I had told my friend Helen over lunch about what I discovered, and I was going to commit suicide.

"I won't see you Monday, I will be gone," I said. Helen just laughed at me thinking I was joking. Even Helen did not know how distraught I was feeling.

I knew I was serious and it was all planned. I had bought the largest bottle of Aspirin I could find. My head was spinning. I could no longer be treated by people the way that I was. This was my only way out.

As his mother left for Bingo she said, "I don't know what time he will be in. I am staying at my sisters tonight."

I sat in the lounge, put the TV on–it was ten to ten. I started shoving these pills down. I just drifted away and I remember my eyes feeling heavy. Even though I knew deep in my heart this was not the answer to my problems, I was finding a sort of peace. I felt in control of myself.

The next thing I knew I was in a room with no doors. There were two forms that appeared to be angels with white gowns on. They looked like they had head-dresses on but these were actually their auras. They looked like nuns to me.

"Where am I?" I asked.

"You have passed over, and you are on the other side.

You are not staying!" They forcefully said.

"Why? I don't want to go back there," I painfully replied.

"You are in the halls of healing. You are here for a little

time to heal. We will show you around and you can gain some understanding of what the other side is all about." Their voices were ever so gentle as they spoke to me.

"When it is your time and you pass over, you come to the halls of healing until your soul and spiritual body recover. The time you spend here depends on each individual soul and the experiences they have had on earth."

I remember the corridor. There were hundreds of people all passing by, young, old, men, women, children, babies, women holding babies. I couldn't believe there were so many people.

I said, "Who are all these people?"

"These are all the people that have passed over, they have been in the first healing room, where some healing has been completed and they are now moving on to the next level."

"What is the next level?" I enquired.

"The Lord has many floors to his mansion," was the unusual reply I received.

"What does that mean?"

"It just means there are many layers and levels of healing and learning and that is up to each individual soul as to when each level is completed."

"Over on this side, anything that you can imagine, you can have. You can be what ever age you want to be, that house, that garden, that car are all here for you. For example, if you always wanted to learn the piano and never did, on this other side in the halls of music, you can actually learn with no pressure. Souls of great musicians and composers such as Mozart don't reincarnate. They stay in the halls of music and assist those souls in their musical development, who when they go back will have those abilities in that next lifetime. The same

is for abilities in areas such as writing or painting, in fact any area that a soul will require when back on Earth.

"While I am here can you tell me is there any hell, as when we are on Earth we are told there is a hell?"

"You have just said it, Hell on Earth and you live through that each day until you come over here to what you people call Heaven."

"Well," I said, "What happens to suicide people?"

"They go to another area and they are counselled and talked to about what they have done. There is no condemnation to hell. It is up to them whether they choose to work through their own hell which is within their own selves. The quicker they do it the more they can help their family in their grieving process."

"Why then, am I supposed to survive this?"

"You have not finished your work on earth. You are just having a bit of a rest. You will go back and you will complete what you have set out to do. This is an opportunity for you to learn more and you will remember this so you can use it further along in your life."

The next thing I knew I was back in his house vomiting. It was about 4am, I had been away for six hours. When I looked at myself in the mirror, I was blue. As I was hanging over the sink vomiting he walked in.

"What are you doing, what are you doing here?" he screamed at me.

"I have been waiting for you. Where have you been?" I managed to get the words out.

"I have been out," he continued screaming at me. "What is wrong with you?"

"I tried to kill myself. I wanted you to find me dead!"

"Get out of here," he said and pushed me out of the door, throwing my things after me.

After that things didn't get any better. We continued on as we always had. His mother knew our relationship wasn't right and one day, she took me aside and said,

"You would be very silly to marry him. He brings different girls home here at night."

Here again was the warning and here again I didn't listen. It was six weeks before our wedding and all I wanted was to be married. I had my wedding dress, people were coming from America. It is always interesting how we have situations put in front of us to stop us in our tracks and actually listen to our inner voice. I heard through a friend that Roy went out with another girl when he said he was going out with friends. Finally I confronted him and told him that I knew he was seeing someone else.

"Yes I have been and now I am going to marry her. I have met her parents and we are engaged." Deep down, I had known that I would never marry him, but it was still a huge shock.

He did marry her and I was devastated. I felt so unbelievably alone and there was no sympathy from home. All they could say was "we told you so" and all I wanted was someone to say it was okay and to hug and console me. For the four years that I had been going out with him I had been saving madly. I had a substantial amount in the account. It wasn't long before he phoned me and told me that he was having half of the money that I had saved. We had never lived together so he had no rights to it. We were to meet by the bank where my account was located. Like a fool I went down to meet him. The next thing I knew he was behind me with a knife in my back.

"What are you doing?" I wanted to turn around as I asked this but I was too scared to move.

"We are going to the bank. You are going to draw all that money out and give it all to me. If you don't that is the end of you!"

I was petrified. I knew he would not hesitate as I knew he would have taken drugs that morning and he was capable of anything. So all the way over to the bank in my head I was saying "What am I going to do I can't give him all this money." Then I heard Spirit say,

"Put the wrong date on it; put the wrong date on the cheque."

So I wrote it out for all the money I had in my account with totally the wrong date on the cheque. I gave it to him and said,

"I have to go back to work," and got out of there as quick as I could.

I ran all the way back to work. The phone rang.

"You are dead! I know what you have done." It was him.

At the end of the day I crept out the back way to avoid him. Everywhere I went I would search the crowds to make sure he wasn't there. I didn't see him for a few months until I was out on the town at a pub with a person from work. I went up to the bar to get a drink and as I turned around I banged into Roy with his new fiancée. On her finger was my engagement ring, the ring that I had given back when we finished. They left soon after. I was relieved and started to enjoy myself.

Thirty minutes later he was back, alone. He had a furious look on his face as he dragged me off the stool at the bar. I was pulled onto the floor, where he kicked me and then pushed me down the stairs. Nobody helped me. Roy continued to hit me and then rammed me into the wall. It was with so much force that I went flying backwards. I was out cold.

"You have got to get up. He will kill you if you don't. You have to get up." Spirit was here.

I don't know where I got the strength from. I staggered up. I had no skin on my knees from the dragging. I had a bleeding nose. I got my fist and hit him with so much force in his face, and then I kicked him between the legs.

"You are dead, you are over that balcony," he yelled out in pain.

All I remember is running away, getting into a taxi and going home. I lay in bed with my clothes on and my mother came into the room.

"What are you in bed with your clothes on for?" my mother said horribly to me, "What have you done?"

I turned around, I couldn't see out of my eye. There was blood all over me. I got up and had a shower. I could hardly move I was so sore and the pain was incredible. I had footprints in the shape of his boot on me. I know I should have pressed charges but I didn't have the confidence, and my family didn't support me in this.

After a few years, I met Roy's sister in the street. She could tell me that he was still married to the same woman, but she was living a life of hell. She gets beaten often. If I had married Roy I wouldn't be where I am now. He would have killed me or I literally would have killed him and ended up in prison.

That would've been me. Thank God I escaped.

Steve – My Soul Mate

"It is time to start living again. You have to put Roy behind you." Spirit repeatedly said to me.

I had become very withdrawn since I finished with Roy and I didn't speak to anyone. Every day I would be terrified in case I saw him. On the way to and from work I still continued to search faces in the crowds and I would often turn to see if he was following me. Arriving home from work I would go into my room and shut the door. I did not go out socially for over a year even though I was asked.

Spirit continued to be persistent,

"Come on you have to go out, you have to go out."

It was a cold winter night, November the first 1975, when my friend again asked me to go out. It was raining, cold, we had no transport and I was really against going. Spirit continued to encourage me,

"It will be good for you, you need to go out."

We went to a number of different pubs and ended up in a nightclub. My friend was having a great time dancing with a guy while I was standing there alone, unsure of how to behave as it had been a long time since I had been out without a boyfriend. I was totally unsociable and I did give the appearance of wanting to leave.

"I am going home," I eventually said to my friend.

"Don't go home, he's got a friend."

The next thing I knew I was being taken by my arm and introduced to this guy called Steven. I didn't connect at this point that this was the Steven that Spirit had talked to me long ago when I had first met Roy. When I was with Roy and Spirit would tell me I was to marry a Steven I used to say to them,

"You've got the name mixed up. I'm going to marry Roy," I would say not wanting to listen to Spirit.

Steven and I talked for a while but I was still keen to go home. A couple of weeks later I heard that he had been asking a friend about me so I decided to be bold and phone him to ask him out.

"Hi Steven," I said on the phone, "Sue here. Do you fancy going out tomorrow night?"

"I'll see. What is your phone number?" Came the curt brief reply and down went the phone.

My brother had been listening and began mocking me for asking someone out. I did wonder if I had made a mistake.

The next day he did phone me back and said he would meet me in a couple of hours. Panic set in. I had long hair and was two hours long enough to get myself ready? There was a feeling inside of me about Steven that I knew I had to follow up. We met at a bar on this first date and straight away I knew what that feeling was now. He was my soul mate.

It was so overwhelming. His energy was so beautiful. He didn't put any limitations on me, he was gentle, he was funny, and he made me laugh. I had to learn to trust that someone could be kind, as I had not known that my entire life. By Christmas, seven weeks after our very first meeting, and four weeks after our first date, he asked me to marry him. I told him I had been engaged before and what had happened. I said to him if we are still together on July 31st, my birthday in six months time, we will get engaged. Well we did get engaged on the 31st July and we went on a cruise to celebrate. We married on the 5th of February 1977.

"This is the Steven we have been telling you about all your life," Spirit whispered in my ear.

In England people do not get married in February, as it is freezing and usually snowing. My mother could not understand my reasoning and asked me,

"Why do you have to always be different? Why can't you be like a normal person and get married in July?"

"Probably because I am not normal!" I will never forget saying to her. She looked at me very strangely.

A terrific snowstorm filled the week leading up to our wedding. The snow was so thick you needed a shovel to clear it and it was near impossible to get out of the house.

"Look at this weather. People are not going to come to your wedding!" My mother would say every time she looked out the window. I started to get really down about it.

I continually said to Spirit, "Please Spirit don't, please

don't let the weather be like this. Please be fine by Saturday."

As a small child, I used to talk to the weather all the time. I would sit out in the back garden all wrapped up looking up at the sky.

"Who ever is listening up there, if you give me a bit more sunshine I promise I won't want any more. Just five minutes is all I ask." It used to happen. The sun would come out and the clouds would clear. So on the Friday night before the wedding, I was lying in bed, and as I heard the heavy rain. I said,

"Spirit please let it be nice for tomorrow."

The next morning when I awoke all the snow had gone. It was frosty but the sky was blue. I got up excited, knowing that I was marrying a wonderful man and that I would be finally leaving this house and all that I had endured for twenty three years.

It was a funny sort of morning preparing for my wedding. There was little interest shown by anyone in the house and at one point when my zip was stuck I had to struggle with it all by myself. When my makeup was done and I was waiting to go to the church I was hoping that somebody in this family would come in and say I looked beautiful or even a few words of encouragement would have been sufficient. I was left disappointed. However I did feel I looked beautiful and within me I was really excited. I walked out to the waiting limousine and drove up the street a little way and then back to the church which was right next door. My mother thought I was pretentious and she was embarrassed but this was my day and I wanted all the trimmings that go with a wedding. My father gave me away, and I loved getting married to Steve.

The next day after I was married, we went home to pick up my clothes for our honeymoon and no one spoke to me or Steve. They looked at me as though you are married now, and you don't belong here. I felt like my heart had broken and I couldn't put it back together again. I got my things and went downstairs and after saying goodbye and receiving little response back Steve said to me,

"It is not right; you have done nothing wrong in marrying me and moving onto a new life."

Spirit spoke to me as we walked down the path to the waiting taxi,

"You will find the peace that you are looking for in your marriage to Steven."

As we were young and had very little money Steve's parents offered us accommodation with them. Here I was in a loving home and yet I felt homesick for the horrible old ways of my parents' home. It was the only way I knew. Maybe if I had felt that my mother and father were happy for me and there had been some closure I would've felt different? Even though I had freedom and there was nobody telling me what to do, it was all very peculiar. My system was struggling as it seemed to want to find its way back into that old energy feeling. Spirit continually reassured me that all would be well.

Eventually money started to come in as I had a good job with a big finance company and Steve had just completed an engineering apprenticeship. We decided to apply for a council house and we moved into an apartment in a complex, 14 storeys up. It was a pretty miserable place to live, we had no car or phone but as there was only Steve and I, we managed. We had been married for nine months and were not intending to have a baby when I became pregnant unexpectedly. I phoned my parents up as I guess I was looking for approval or some excitement about the first grandchild. Dad was out in the garden and I spoke to my mother first. I was thrilled and told her the news.

"You wait till your father hears about this?" What a strange reply this was from my mother.

Dad came on the phone next.

"You are going to be a grandfather." I said with much excitement,

"Oh, okay, bye" and that was it.

My first pregnancy was not going well and I feared for my unborn child. I had been on serious antibiotic medication for an infection when I became pregnant and I was worried that I had harmed my unborn baby. The doctor said I had to make a decision whether I kept this baby or not. As I lay in bed that night I silently asked,

"Do I keep or let this baby go?"

"Everything will be alright. You are to keep this child."

I blinked my eyes as I saw Jesus and his brilliant energy that was in the room. He had come to comfort me and He gave me overwhelming peace that everything was going to be alright. These were the words I needed to hear and so without telling Steve how I had made a decision, we went ahead with the pregnancy. At five months pregnant I went over to visit my parents but they found it difficult to look at me. Their whole response to me was one of; I was filthy and I had done something really bad. I could not share with them my feelings of worry about my unborn child. Even though I trusted the message I had received earlier on I still carried an underlying fear and concern. A week before my baby was due Jesus came to me again.

"All will be well," He lovingly reassured me again.

Spirit had shown me early on in my life as I had sat outside in the deck chair in the garden, that I would be fortunate to have *"three children and they will all be girls."*

Eventually Samantha was born and Steve and I were elated. My mother came to visit me in the hospital and after she had momentarily looked at the baby she said to me,

"You look disgusting. You are so fat. You look as though you are having another baby."

I had put on a lot of weight since I had married and while I was pregnant. The midwife had assured me that I would lose it but the only comments I seemed to hear were my mother's.

This really affected me and when I came out of hospital I wouldn't eat, I wouldn't drink and I started to lose a lot of weight. We had decided to take Samantha one Saturday afternoon to visit my parents. I was searching in the airing cupboard for a cloth when I found my wedding dress. I tried it on and I could actually fit it again. I had lost about twenty five kilograms. I went down stairs to show Steve.

"Look at this I have got it on," I was very excited.

My mother looked at me and didn't say a word at how I had lost my weight.

I sadly went upstairs and took it off. That was the last time I saw that dress. My mother had given it away to the Op Shop.

"Do you fancy going to New Zealand?" Steve asked as he lifted his head from the newspaper.

"There is a job here advertised for an engineer in New Zealand all-expenses-paid."

"Where's that?" Geography wasn't my strong point, and all I knew about was New Zealand lamb and New Zealand butter. Steve wasn't sure where New Zealand was either but we both decided it had to be better than the life we were living. I had given up work to be at home with Samantha and all day I was usually stuck in the apartment, making me feel like I was in a prison. The young people often stopped the lifts from working and, being fourteen stories up, it was impossible to get out. My ties to my parents were fading fast as they never came to visit us as apparently we lived too far away. I had become very depressed and I knew we had nothing to lose.

Steve went for the interview and he was away all day. The company were looking for someone who was prepared to change their whole life, move to New Zealand and bring their family up there. He had another interview and from over fifty applicants he was offered the job. From the time he accepted the job, it took another six months to get to New Zealand. We put on a going away party, as I had many aunts and uncles and cousins to say goodbye to. My parents and brother and sister came and even though it gave everyone the appearance of us being a normal family there were no tears shed from either side. We left England on the Christmas of 1979 and arrived in New Zealand on Boxing Day.

Sue and Steve's wedding day, 5th February 1977.

Sue's with her first born, Samantha, 1978.

A New Country

We arrived with just two suitcases as when we left the airport in England we had to dump a lot of our clothes and pushchair, as we did not have enough money to pay the extra in overweight charges.

"What have we come to?" I said to Steve when we reached Wellington. The houses were all perched on the hills and they looked so different from the houses I knew. There were few shops and they were all closed. We were met by a couple from the engineering firm where Steve was to work and they took us to a place called Wainuiomata, where we would live for the next twenty seven years.

The house we rented was furnished but had no necessities such as linen, blankets or towels, so we were to sleep that first night with our coats on, on bare mattresses. As we began unpacking our two suitcases, Steve said,

"I notice you have left most of my clothes behind not yours!"

He should've known I couldn't be without my clothes.

We could not buy anything as in 1979 in New Zealand the shops were not open over the Christmas break. Here we were in a strange country, with a young baby and feeling completely miserable and wondering what we had done.

When you arrive in a strange country, you have no concept of the lifestyle, the culture or the language and you can certainly get into comical situations. After a pretty sleepless night the couple came back the next morning and said they would take us to the dairy to get what we needed. Steve and I looked at each other and we mouthed "dairy?" and I whispered, "I think it is a cow shed!" We presumed we were going to get some milk! Maybe here in New Zealand that's how you buy your milk, straight from the farm.

We drove around for what seemed like ages and finally the man said, "This is it."

"A shop! This is a corner store," I exclaimed.

"What did you think it was?" he looked with amazement written all over his face.

"I thought we were going to a farm or something to get some milk," I embarrassingly replied.

A few days later, another couple came around to meet us. He would be working with Steve and would give him a ride to work each day. When they were going, they said,

"We will see you later," so I sat up all night waiting for them to come back.

It was getting later and later and Steve could wait up no longer.

"They are not coming back, I'm going to bed," he said.

"I can't, they said they are coming back later."

We didn't see them for four days, and when they did come back I said to the woman,

"Where were you?"

"What do you mean?" she asked with a puzzled look on her face.

"When you last visited us, you said you would see us later, but you didn't come back. I waited up till twelve!"

Well they laughed and laughed. There were so many sayings and ways of life in New Zealand that I had to get used to.

Learning to say "Wainuiomata" with my broad Birmingham accent and even remembering the name of this strange new town was proving to be difficult for me. I slipped back into an old habit and changed it to something I could remember.

"Why buy a tomato," I would mumble when people asked me where I was staying. They would come back at me with, "Oh Wainuiomata," and I would very quickly reply to the affirmative.

As I had grown up not knowing a lot of kindness, I often mistook people's so-called caring as kindness without looking at their underlying purpose and intentions. This meant I often said 'yes' without thinking things through as I was just happy to receive some form of kindness. One of the couples that we first met when we arrived in New Zealand asked us if we would like to stay with them to save some more money. We moved out of our flat and moved in with them. It wasn't long before we discovered that she really wanted us there to increase her own bank balance. We had to pay to watch television; we paid for all the electricity and gas, most of the food, so it ended up that we weren't saving anything at all.

On Saturday mornings, when the two men went to work I would get up feed Samantha and her two children while she lay in bed. I would clean all the house, do the washing, do the ironing and when she heard the men come back at 12 o'clock she would jump out of bed, and appear as though she had been up for hours doing all the house work. I am sure the husband thought I didn't do anything.

It was time to leave there and rent our own house again. Our furniture was soon to arrive from England so we moved into an empty house. We sat on the floor, the three of us slept on one bed but we did get some cutlery and plates. Being in New Zealand was beginning to upset me and I was growing to dislike this new country of ours. I was becoming incredibly lonely and so I decided to look for a job. I heard about a job in a factory, and even though I had never worked in a factory before, as I had always done office work, I decided to give it a go. It would help to have the extra money to buy a house that we dreamed of.

Samantha was put into childcare and I hadn't been there long, when one day the head teacher said they were having a party and would I bring a plate. I went home and said to Steve,

"I have to take a plate to the childcare. It's funny them

asking for a plate."

"Probably the kids break them and their stocks have run a little low," Steve offered.

"Do you think I should take a knife, fork and a spoon as well?"

"It wouldn't hurt."

So I went out and bought a matching set, and I walked into the nursery on the night of the party, and I said to the woman,

"There you go, there is the plate and a few other bits and pieces. I have put her name on the bottom of the plate. If she breaks it, it doesn't matter."

All the women looked at me, and they all burst out laughing.

"What is funny?" I asked as the head teacher couldn't talk for laughing. I got a bit annoyed.

Not knowing how to handle this situation I said, "Do you want more plates?"

She finally got herself together and said, "It's a plate with food on it!"

I certainly was having difficulty with all the different sayings and this was yet another experience to add to my growing list.

The factory job was in a cigarette factory. Everybody would gather at morning tea, and they would all be smoking, which I found very difficult as I was a non-smoker. It was hard and heavy work with a lot of stress and strain but we needed the money for our house so I was determined to stay as long as I could. One day as I was standing next to the machine I felt horrible. It was like everything was in slow motion, and then I collapsed. Slowly I came around and I heard them say,

"We need to phone her next of kin she has had a stroke."

The ambulance took me to hospital. My whole left side had been affected and I couldn't move my arm or leg, my eye wouldn't open and my face had fallen. Dye was put through my body to check where the blockage was in my brain.

"Had I had any headaches before?" was the first question I was asked after these tests were completed.

All the headaches and the blackouts that I had as a child and nothing was ever done about them, flashed before me. Apparently this problem had been with me for a very long time and was just waiting to happen. I had difficulty with walking after this and had to re-learn to walk properly again. I was told that for the rest of my life I would need to learn to deal with stress and to stay clear of situations that would put strain on myself.

We scrimped and saved and managed to get enough money together to put a deposit on a house. At this time I was also able to change jobs. This settled me for a while and then I discovered I was pregnant again. We decided I would stay home and look after the two girls.

It wasn't long before I was pregnant again. Straight after the birth, Sarah, my third daughter was put in her cot and I was taken back to the ward. As I lay there sleeping and resting I heard an old familiar voice in my head,

"Wake up and see to your baby."

My eyes were opening just as the nurse came in.

"Go back to sleep because your baby is asleep." The nurse insisted.

"Don't leave her now, pick her up. You must attend to her now." Spirit persisted.

She was a strange colour.

"Undo her nappy," they said.

When I undid her nappy there was all this blood. They hadn't put a clip on her umbilical cord properly. She was haemorrhaging. Spirit saved her life.

My mother decided to come to New Zealand to visit us and to meet her new grandchildren. This show of motherly love was a huge surprise for me. It proved to be yet another unhappy experience with her, as New Zealand was so different and even 'the apples weren't good enough as they weren't the same as back home in England.' My self-esteem plummeted as again I went back to being the little girl and felt totally incompetent with her around. The continual seeking of approval from her was still with me, and when she did return home I would phone her up but there was very little conversation to be had. They were either busy or doing something 'important'.

A Visit to a So-called Clairvoyant

Slowly I developed some friends in the neighbourhood; some were mothers of my daughter's friends, others were from work. Because of the huge change in lifestyle and the overriding need to just exist in this new country, listening to Spirit and contacting the other side had taken a back seat in my life. Out of the blue a friend asked me to go with her for a reading with a so-called clairvoyant. Excitement grew as the time came nearer and I thought of what I might be told. As soon as I opened the door I knew I had made a mistake, it felt evil, but there was no going back. I sat in this woman's living room and my friend went in first. While sitting there I saw this elderly lady come in and I began talking to her when all of a sudden she walked straight through the wall. I realised Spirit was appearing to me in an extremely solid form. Spirit then said to me,

"She appeared to you to remind you that you have the gift of seeing." So much had been put on hold while I was adjusting to my new life as a mother and a new life in New Zealand.

It was my turn next. I cautiously went into this woman's room. She was dressed all in black. She looked me up and down for what seemed like an eternity and then said to me,

"You have very special gifts. I know you see Spirit."

I decided not to say anything and just see what she had to say to me.

"I hold a circle at night and it is very exclusive and you only get an invite at my discretion."

It hit me, this woman was a witch and she was talking about a witches coven. I had seen some of the books on witchcraft and voodoo that she had in her bookshelf in her waiting room and it all fell into place.

"I want to teach you many things and with the many talents that you have you will fill the last spot in the circle."

I could see a man in Spirit standing behind her and eventually it got the better of me, so I told her I could see her late husband and I was even able to tell her how he was killed.

This excited her and she launched into telling me more about her circle and was insisting I join.

"It is not right, do not do this." Spirit started to tell me, but before Spirit could tell me again, I was giving my telephone number to her.

I did not know how to say no and I didn't want to upset anyone face-to-face. As my friend Linda and I were driving home, she asked me what I had thought of my session.

"She has asked me to join her circle," I told her.

"There is something about her I didn't like. I wouldn't

go if I was you as she was very strange," Linda responded.

Another warning and yet a few days later I agreed to go to my first circle evening. I would tell her on the night that I would not be continuing with the circle. Little did I know that this was the worst decision that I could make. There were eight of us in the circle, seven women and one man. The rules were given out; we were to be on time always and there was to be no telling of what goes on in the circle to anybody. At no time during the evening, were we ever to break the circle after it had started. We were not to mix or even talk to anybody from the circle outside this evening. She talked with so much authority it frightened me. You will remain in the circle for as long as I want you to be.

I was extremely scared of this woman and could not say I would not be returning. I actually went back two more times.

"You don't know what you are dealing with. You will learn what the dark side is," Spirit warned me again.

On the third night I knew I had to say I was leaving the circle. I would do it at the end. The evening began with a meditation that developed into a form of chanting. A very black negative feeling around me emerged. Something touched me on the right side of my neck. I was extremely frightened and I broke the circle.

"There is something evil in this room and it touched my neck!" I stood up saying in a loud voice.

"What ever is coming to me is not nice." This scared a number of others in the circle. There was definitely an evil energy in that room.

The 'witch' took control of the others in the group, and began turning them against me. I left.

In the following days I felt paranoid and I didn't feel me. There was something inside of me that didn't feel right. My friend, Linda, commented to me how my personality had changed and she suggested I go to see someone for some help.

"Have you been in a circle?" was the first question I was asked by the healer.

"Someone has put a curse on you. Please go as I don't want that energy in here. Contact this person as they may be able to help you."

This frightened me even more and I quickly organised a meeting with the very gentle Indian man she recommended. He could tell me that they were still working on me to break me, they were very powerful and they wanted me under their control. He told me to wear my cross and gave me some holy water for protection. I contacted the 'witch' and told her I was not coming back to the circle.

"Don't think you are getting away from me, nobody walks away from me. Just be warned it has not stopped yet," she said down the phone. "You will come over to our side."

I stayed strong and with the help of Arch Angel Michael, the dark energy eventually left me.

"You were being tested," Spirit told me. *"In the future, when you come up against the dark side and evil, you will be strong. You will not be frightened of anything. That woman had tremendous power and if only she had used it for good.*

Always remember that good conquers evil."

My soul was dented and this experience stopped me from listening and having anything to do with Spirit for quite some time.

Steve and Sue two years after arriving in New Zealand.

Searching for Peace

After I had been in New Zealand for nine years I became very down and all I wanted to do was go home to England. I was seeing a counsellor, and after I told her about my childhood she suggested the only way to get over this was to face my mother. By this point, Steve had risen to be the manager at the firm that brought him out to New Zealand and he was doing really well.

"I have to go back. If you don't come I will go by myself," I sobbed.

"If that's what you really want. Then we will go," Steve said.

Steve left his job and we sold our house to finance the trip as we decided to go for the year. To help the people buy our house, we left some money in it. My brother and Steve's Dad met us at the airport and we went back to my parent's place where we were to stay initially. I found my mother in the kitchen preparing sandwiches to welcome us. My father came in and said to me,

"Look what your mother has done for you, you had better appreciate it. Your mother has slaved all day over this!"

What had I returned to? I had only just arrived, and I

meekly said in a quiet voice,

"Yes I do. I haven't seen you in eight years and is that all you can say?"

I had bought each of them a present; one was a watch for my mother. She picked it up and said, "You know, I don't wear watches. There you go," and gave it back to me.

It really hurt me and I realised, things hadn't changed and our relationship had actually grown worse. How was I going to cope with the five of us living with them?

We had transferred some money across from New Zealand to England but as it was Christmas time we could not get our money until after the New Year holiday had ended. We were to pay board which we had no problem with. As it wasn't there immediately in front of them it was growing into a contentious issue and I assured them we would pay as soon as the money came through.

Having a house full of people was building up a house full of tension. My unmarried sister was still living at home and one day I heard my mother and her talking about me in the bedroom. I wanted to burst into the room and ask why they were doing this to me and what had I done wrong.

My head over-ruled my heart and I realised I couldn't burst in, as we had three children and nowhere to go. After all these years, here I was a grown woman with children and yet I still could not speak my mind and say how I felt. The best way of dealing with this I thought was just to get out the house and try and work through it. I got up really early, left the house without saying anything and just walked around and around all day. Nobody knew where I was and it was night-time before I returned home.

When I got home, Steve asked me, looking worried,

"Where have you been?"

"I just had to get out of this house. I couldn't stand it any longer." The tears begin to well up.

My mother attempted to say she was worried, and I just replied calmly,

"I tell you now, as soon as we get our money, I am out of here. We are out of here. We will find a place as we are not staying here any more."

I finally told Steve how they had been saying awful things about us and how we had been eating all their food. The next few weeks were very difficult as we would go out with the children and when we came home, they would not speak to us. The final straw was one night when my father was out, my mother started to do the things to my children that she used to do to me. I was standing at the top of the stairs, and I heard her say to Samantha, my eldest daughter to my next daughter Sacha,

"Go on, say to your sister how stupid she is."

I came downstairs, furious and said,

"How dare you say that to her, how dare you do that to my children."

"I don't know what you're talking about, there's something wrong with you," was her ever-so-innocent reply.

"I have been listening to you outside the door. You

are playing Samantha against Sacha exactly the way you did with my brother and I," I screamed.

Thank goodness the money from New Zealand came through. We found a house that was fully furnished and we stayed there for the year. The reason I had wanted to come back to England was to hopefully find some peace by discovering a mother-daughter relationship, but what I did find was that I didn't belong in England. My family visited us just two times in that whole year and when we were leaving my mother came to the airport crying.

"Don't bother crying, those aren't real tears. Why would you want to cry about me and my children with the way that you have treated us?"

She stopped and looked at me as I said this with so much strength and conviction,

"You will never see your grandchildren again."

She never did.

Spirit reflected to me,

"By words or deeds that we bitterly bestow on to another soul, sometime with our life here on Earth we will feel and again experience those hurtful words and deeds. They will be given to us from another soul and we will not know the time or place or from whom until it happens."

* * * *

We came back to New Zealand, and we were worse off than we were before. We landed at Auckland airport, with three children, three suitcases, and nowhere to live. I felt awful because Steve had left a good job and all because I had to go back and try and find the love that I craved, but now realised was never going to happen. This was the lowest point that I had ever experienced in my life. We had no money and the money we had left in our previous house was not available to us, as the new owners would not pay us back as they had separated.

I was fortunate to have a friend in Auckland and so we stayed with them for four days until we managed to get a cheap rental car to get back to Wellington. Now we were in Wellington, with three children, three suitcases and no money! Luckily I had another friend in Wellington and she kindly put us up for a few days and we slept on the floor.

Before I went back to England, I had worked as a production manager at a local carpet factory where I met a lovely man called Bill Cook. We had become friends and I used to visit him often with the girls and they looked upon him as a grandfather. I decided to contact him to see if we could stay for a little while and luckily he said we could stay as long as we liked and he would love to have the children there as well.

It was a pretty desperate situation as we had no jobs, no money and we could not find a house to rent. Every evening, I would scour the paper looking for a job. Finally I saw a job advertised at a stockbroker's and with the power of positive thinking, three interviews and many questions I was given the job.

My hours were from twelve midnight to seven in the morning working the shift by myself. We were able to move out from Bill's house as we finally found a place to rent that was fully furnished. Steve decided to work for himself doing maintenance work and after two years, we had saved up enough money to build our own house.

Emerging Abilities

Moving into our newly built home brought a lot of stability into my life. My three beautiful daughters were each growing with their own talents and gifts of psychic ability. Creating games to teach the girls how to develop their gifts without them knowing became the means for me in assisting their psychic abilities.

"If you know which colour the sweet is in my hand, you can have it," I would often say. Telepathically I would be giving out the message and they would have to concentrate and practice getting what I was sending. I would extend the game by getting different colours in my hands and asking them to hold my hand and see if they could sense what the colour was.

We were a happy family and I vowed and declared I would treat my daughters how I wished my parents could have treated me. I have learnt to love and value my children and the gifts I know they have been blessed with.

"Your daughters do have the gift," Spirit told me, *"They have chosen you in this lifetime to assist them with their abilities."*

As the girls grew they started to see Spirit and learnt to accept that they had this ability, whereas I knew as a young child I had this ability but could not talk to anyone about it.

"The school teacher was yellow today Mum." My youngest daughter, Sarah would say when she came home from school. Sarah was seeing the teacher's Aura and so we would discuss how the teacher had been in the classroom that day as it was all reflected in the colour of her energy field.

My girls were born very fortunate as they have a mother who believed in what they were seeing, sensing and hearing. Spirit sees the children that are Spiritually open and psychic, as beams of light. It's a bit like moths around a bright light. More and more children are now being born who are open Spiritually and can see Spirit and it is essential to treasure these wonderful abilities these children have.

When your family are open and able to see Spirit, all sorts of happenings can occur as the other side is attracted to this signal that is going out. I often tell my children you have to trust what has been given to you. At the time you may not understand the messages that you are given, but in time it will happen. You may be requested to pass on a message to the appropriate person and this also you must do. Realising that it is not all just in their heads and Spirit is actually openly in contact with them is the most difficult part of learning to trust that Spirit is there.

Sometimes when Spirit appears it can frighten the girls and I have had phone calls at all times of the day and night from them but it is learning how to deal with the situation and asking them to go to the light. It is important that the girls maintain these gifts and grow with it. Just as I have a contract, I know the girls do also.

One night I came home late and Samantha had been looking after the two younger girls. As soon as I came in I heard the petrified voice of Samantha call out,

"Is that you Mum? There's something in the passage and it looks like Sarah but it is not. She is in bed. I think it is a ghost!"

I went into the hallway and there was this ghost girl, the splitting image of Sarah.

A mischievous grin came over the little girl's face as she walked through the wall confirming it definitely was not Sarah.

"She won't hurt you," I reassured Samantha, "I will ask her to go to the light." However this little girl was not about to leave.

The next week a friend came around, the door to the hallway was open and I was in the kitchen. My friend said to me,

"Sarah's up, she's playing about and popping her head around the doorway."

"No, that's not Sarah that's our ghost!" Well the look on my friend's face said it all.

This little Spirit girl started to become very naughty.

It was a Sunday night. The TV remote and lighter were always left on the table. Steve came back into the TV room and asked where the remote was. Well we searched that house and the remote was nowhere to be found. Then his lighter went. His watch went. I knew it was the Spirit of this little girl that was with us. Steve was becoming totally frustrated.

Next my washing machine overflowed and I called the plumber in. He found in the workings of the machine this huge old fashioned hairgrip; a hairgrip that was used in olden times. We certainly did not have any hairgrips of this sort. The following week, the tumble dryer stopped going and there inside was another big hairgrip. This was beginning to cost me money.

"I don't mind you being here with us," I said with utter frustration to the little Spirit girl, "but you must behave. You must bring back now, all the things you have taken and stay away from our machines."

I don't know where Spirit took these things to, but they did all come back. I have a feeling they go into another dimension. She eventually did go and we never heard from her again.

Loved ones can also visit us at the most inappropriate times. Sacha, my second daughter, rang me one night quite hysterical. She had been taking a shower when out of the corner of her eye she saw a man standing there. Of course she screamed, got out of there very quickly and phoned me. At first she thought it was a real person but as she moved 'he' disappeared. I explained to her it was Spirit and actually a past relative that had come to visit. She asked,

"Is he a pervert Mum?"

"Spirit does not come to look at all the everyday things we are doing as that does not interest them. 'He' obviously wanted to communicate with you but picked totally the wrong place and wrong time. Next time this happens tell him to come back again when it is a more suitable for you."

Sue's daughters Samantha (aged 10), Sarah (aged 4) and Sacha (aged 6).

The more I worked with the girls the more the door was opening again to my own spiritual gifts. I couldn't get enough new knowledge and I attended a weekend class with a friend to learn Reiki. When the teacher began talking about Reiki, it just resonated with me instantly as the answers to the questions that I had been asking myself were being answered. After the introduction we went into meditation.

I had only been in the meditation for a short while when this Japanese man came in. He had a samurai sword and behind him was a path leading up to a huge building, much like a castle. He said to me,

"You see that path, you will walk that path and you will reach the top of that path. You will enter that building."

When we came back out of the meditation and it was my turn to describe what I had seen the teacher looked at me and then picked up a book to show me a picture.

"That is him," I said excitedly.

"That is who I am going to talk about next. He was the founder of Reiki."

The longer she talked the more I said to myself 'I do that now' and then information came to me and I realised I had been subconsciously doing this for some time.

"You do not take the person's energy on as it is not yours to hold," she explained. "With Reiki you let the energy go to the universe to be healed. You are just a channel."

I shared with the teacher and the class how appropriate this was to hear and of the recent experience with my friend in trying to heal her severe ear infection. For her it went but for me two days later I had the most incredible pain in my ear. I went to the doctors and she said,

"You have got the most terrible infection in your ear, how long have you had this?"

"It just came on."

"There is no way that this could just come on. You must have had it for a long time."

I had taken my friends pain and infection on.

I had been placing my hands on friends for their healing and I was holding onto their energies and not passing it through to the Universe. No wonder at times I felt I was carrying the whole weight of the world on my shoulders.

During the time I was learning Reiki I also began learning massage. Spirit told me the reason I enjoy massage so much is because I love to have the experience of being close to people. This stemmed from never being held and cuddled as a young child.

The Reiki intunements I received over a number of courses leading up to and gaining Reiki Master and the massage I had learnt, grew my healing abilities incredibly. I have learnt to scan a person's body with my hands and feel where the energy is blocked and there my hands will stop. My hands tingle and become extremely hot when combining Massage and Reiki. Every person that I work on now comments on my exceptionally hot hands.

I continued to increase my learning around alternative forms of healing at every opportunity. I was becoming a sponge. Magnetic healing was one such form. It is based on feeling the vibration around someone with your hands, discovering where the blockages are, and then visualising a light that will be used in the healing. It is very similar to what I had learnt in Reiki.

The group I attended was held twice a week and I went along with my friend. After the introduction we were split into four groups and one person was to take the lead healers role, another was 'the patient' and the rest of the group were to stand around the massage-type bed. There was to be no touching of the 'patient' on the bed.

My training in Reiki came through on that first night and I began to scan each person who was on the bed as I stood at the side. Even though I could feel where there were blockages in the person's energy and the messages were coming thick and fast, I decided not to give them out. I didn't want anyone to think, 'who does she think she is' I was the new person and other people had been going there for weeks.

It was soon my turn to go next onto the bed and receive magnetic healing. There was one male, and three females, and the male was to be the 'healer.' I closed my eyes and he stood at the back of me and started to place his hands by my head. All of a sudden I started to receive messages that this person was manic depressive and he was on medication. I felt sick and I knew I had to get up off the bed. I quickly sat up.

"Are you on medication?"

He confirmed this and that he was depressed and he was actually a schizophrenic. I could not believe that someone who had schizophrenia was actually working with their energy on me. I always have a policy that if I am not well in any form I will not do any energy healing work. Readings are okay. I just looked at him and said,

"You are still having mood swings. You get very angry."

"I'm trying to control them," was all he could offer.

I was annoyed and upset and I said to the teacher that was taking the class, that I wasn't happy about him laying his hands on me. I told him it was okay for him to watch but no way, should he be laying his hands on people. People need to have an understanding of how energy works and how we transfer our energy knowingly and unknowingly into another object, be it a person, animal or plant.

The teacher listened to what I had to say and moved on to something new for the class. He asked us to all gather around the massage bed.

"I am going to visualise someone on that bed," the teacher said. "You are going to tell me who is on that bed, whether they are male or female and what is the matter with them. So who is going to do it?"

Everyone stood back, and then I felt like a push in my back. It was very clearly from Spirit and the next thing I knew, I was standing at the front of the group and of course I was selected. Nobody knew that I was a Spiritual Psychic Medium.

Standing next to the bed I began to scan it. I could pick up the energy of the person on the bed, but for those in the group there was nothing for them to see, and I began saying,

"It's a female I can feel her feet, this length."

There was not a yes or no from the teacher, as I moved through my assessment.

"She cannot move her legs. She has had a massive injury to her spinal column and she can only move her neck and head. She is in a wheelchair. I feel like she is a paraplegic. She was in an accident. She has actually at the moment got kidney failure. The kidneys are failing."

I wasn't looking at the teacher. I was just looking at the bed. The others in the group didn't know if I was telling the truth or not.

He said, "Anything else?"

"She's in real bad shape. She is actually lucky to be alive."

He looked at me and said, "you're talking about my friend, she is about that tall, she is a paraplegic, she was in a car accident, and her kidneys are failing."

Everyone looked at me in amazement. Spirit had certainly done a great job.

Afterwards he said to me,

"What do you do?"

"As yet nobody knows that I have psychic abilities."

Even though I was asked to return, I just didn't feel right being there.

I still did not have the confidence to make a living out of my developing healing and psychic abilities so I continued to look for so-called normal employment. I began scouring the pages looking to see if there was anything suitable or anything of interest. Taking special care of myself, whether it be makeup or hair or clothes was something I loved doing. Finally there was the perfect job as a manager of a makeup business that could be operated from your home.

After I had the interview in Auckland a friend was getting me to the airport. We were late so while he was parking the car I quickly ran inside but unfortunately I did not see the concrete pillar and I went straight smack into it falling down unconscious. When I came around there was blood pouring out of my eye socket and people had gathered but they seemed to not know what to do. I tried to get up, but fell back down again. As the air hostess from behind the counter came over and began trying to sit me up I was thinking in my head,

"Please don't lift me. I could have a neck or head injury."

Thank goodness a bystander had some knowledge and told the air hostess not to lift me. An ambulance arrived. My friend finally found me and got such a shock to see me lying on the floor. He could tell the ambulance officers who I was as my concussion was bad and I didn't know my name. I was taken to the hospital.

After x-raying me and dressing the wound, I insisted I fly back to Wellington that day. I still don't know how I made it and I certainly received lots of looks as I still had my bloody clothes on. Steve was horrified when he finally picked me up from the airport. I was unable to work as I had a head injury and this lead to days when I was extremely depressed and had difficulty getting out of bed.

It was lunchtime and as I was contemplating getting up but seemed to be drifting in and out of sleep. I thought I heard Samantha and her girlfriend come home. The door opened, and then I heard them come up the hallway and to my bedroom door. They seemed to be laughing at me and I called out,

"Why are you laughing at me? Why are you being like this?"

They appeared and they didn't seem to have their school uniforms on. 'Samantha' said,

"Look at you, you are pathetic and I have brought my friend with me to see you like this!" I couldn't understand it.

At this moment I heard Spirit say,

"Take no notice of them. Take no notice of them. Look into their eyes. You will see they are evil. It is not Samantha."

These lower level beings were certainly in my energy space, but in my state I still could not connect with what Spirit was telling me.

"Why haven't you been at school Samantha?" I asked her when I saw her in the afternoon. "Why did you bring your friend around to laugh at me?"

"Mum you are frightening me. I have been at school all day and I definitely didn't come home," she replied.

For some reason, these lower energies were visiting me in the appearance of my family. It was the eyes that were most horrible and the eyes are the windows to the soul. There were no eyes just black balls. There was no soul in these energies.

The pain continued to be severe in my head and one night, as I was going to bed, I thought I am not going to see this night through and I was going to die. I literally felt that something was going to burst in my head as the pain was incredible.

As I lay in bed I said,

"Please I am asking someone out there to help me. I can't stand this pain any longer."

All of a sudden I looked up and I wasn't in my room any more, I was outside. It was like somebody had removed the roof. There, outside were two magnificent angels and I was so close it was like I could touch their wings. They smiled at me and lifted me up. The next day, I had my hearing back, my memory was back and I was feeling so much better. I was healed. I had been suffering from this head injury for six months.

Months after that I was out shopping, and went into a carpet shop even though I didn't want carpet, I was drawn to the shop. Spirit guided me over to this one rug on the wall and said to me,

"Look behind it."

There behind the rug was the most beautiful painting of the two angels that I had seen. I went over to the shop assistant who became confused and said that they didn't stock any paintings. When I showed her the painting, she proceeded to tell me that she had never seen that painting. I really wanted this painting and we finally agreed on the price of fifty dollars. When I got it home on the back of the painting was the title 'The Abduction of the Psyche.'

Coming Out

It was six months since the initial head injury and now, being free of it I began looking for another office job and found one, but it turned out to be only short term.

"By this time tomorrow you will not have a job," Spirit warned me.

I had a sick feeling inside because the money I was earning was helping us with our new house and I really did enjoy the work I was doing.

"It is time now to come out and tell people that you are a psychic medium. You are to begin working with people who we will send to you."

A beautiful calmness came over me and the fears seemed to melt as Spirit shared this with me. Deep inside of me there had always been a hollow and I just knew that this was going to be the start of something wonderful.

My old fears and lack of confidence around my gift quickly came to the surface as the reality of what Spirit had told me sunk in.

Am I able to do this?

Will I know what to say?

Will people come to me?

What will Steve think?

On and on the thoughts began to spin around in my head. I knew I had this gift but would I be capable of going public and earning from it?

I did know that I had developed trust and friendship with the continual guidance I received. I did not know however who Spirit really was or how I had this ability to hear their words. I needed somebody to understand me. Who could I share with, the truth about my gift that I was developing? The only person I knew was Steve and he actually had no real understanding or concept of the depth of my ability.

For all of the 18 years that Steve and I had been married he had no idea that I could see, hear and talk to Spirit as I had kept my gift a secret. I would say things well before they happened and I think he just thought it was coincidence. Life had been a lie regarding Spirit and I knew it was time to come out and tell people. I needed Steve to believe in me and not think that I was mad.

"Sit down Steve," I said, "there is something I have to tell you. It is something I have had all my life." He looked at me with the weirdest look which changed into a very scared look.

"I can talk to dead people on the other side. I see and hear the angels. I know things before they happen. I know if someone has an illness." Out it all came. The floodgates had opened. Everything that I had been bottling up for all these years was now coming out into the open. There was no holding back and there was no hesitation in my voice. I was completely confident in everything that I was telling Steve. The relief in my heart to finally release and share was huge.

Steve sat and listened quietly. There were no interjections. He began to look relieved that this was all that I wanted to tell him and talk about. It was as though Steve knew and accepted that there is more to life than what we physically know.

"I thought you were going to tell me that you had some deadly disease or something and you had never told me," were the first words Steve could say.

I continued on, "Ever since I was little, I have been able to see and talk to people who have passed over who are now on the 'Other Side'. When they appear to me they give me messages and besides seeing and hearing these past loved ones, the angels and even Jesus share their guidance with me. They are all telling me that now is the time for me to come out and do the work that I am meant to be doing. I am to give messages to people who will come to see me from those on the other side. I am to show them that there is more to life than what we know is here on this earth, and that we can talk to and receive guidance from people who have passed over."

"Well good on you, if you think you can do it, go for it then." He had such a wonderful smile on his face as he said this.

I was feeling a lightness in my being that I had never experienced before.

"How are you going to do it?" Was the next question he asked curiously.

In typical fashion, I had not got to that point yet. "I

will get back to you on that one," I mumbled.

Spirit had been preparing me for a long time to have the strength to get to this position in my life and the only way I was going to achieve this was to be mentally strong and to learn to believe in myself. I believe I am tested most days of my life by what I call the darker side that resides in each one of us. This to me is fear of little things such as whether to move house, whether to take a job, whether someone likes us or not, to the fear of big things such as the fear of the unknown in life. We are being continually asked through these tests we encounter as to which way we go and do we choose good or bad. Depression can be the result of the darker side within us.

Enduring the upbringing that I did ensured that there have been many dark episodes in my life. These episodes have tested the belief in myself but have been there to make me stronger. My biggest fear has been that I was unworthy to work for the other side. Each one of us has had experiences in our lives that have created a dark side and at some point in our lives we have to face these darkest fears. This will enable us to move on and grow to be the person that we are meant to be.

I was in my thirties, when I faced my darkest fear. It came in the form of a recurring dream over a number of years. I would go to this very old house with woods all around it and a big circular pebbled driveway. The house was like a mansion and it was empty. I knew in this house there was a dark energy but I was too scared to enter. In my dream I would reach the front door and turn around and leave again.

Even after my real-life children were born I continued to have this dream. The dream had moved up a notch and now we were all living in the mansion. I would tell my girls in the dream as they would look up the stairs to the attic

"Something is up in the attic that you must never ever see. Do not go up."

The years went by and I knew in my waking state that whatever was in that attic in that dream I had to face. I would have to go up the stairs and into the attic. The night arrived when the dream returned. I went up the stairs with my children following and just before I reached the attic door I heard a loud demanding voice say,

"Enter."

"If you want me I will come to you but leave my children alone," I forcefully replied.

I told the girls to go and I tentatively opened the door. I was petrified. Inside the attic was the darker side of me personified as the 'Devil'. The energy in here was huge and I felt very, very small and nothing I had ever known compared to it. I felt totally overpowered and terrified and I was fighting not to go towards it. This was an enormous test to see if I could seek out this dark entity within me and overcome it. If I did not face this energy I would be forever stuck in my powerlessness.

Closer and closer I was being drawn to him and I knew he could read my mind. He knew my fear and all my darkest secrets. Out loud I was saying the Lord's

Prayer as fast as I could as I was being drawn in to this dark mass. It was everything you would hate to happen to you. Then from deep inside of me I began pleading,

"Please God, please God help me."

"Do you think He is going to help you?" the 'Devil' laughed at me.

"You have no hope. You are mine now, and you are going to be mine forever."

He thought it was so funny. These words from the 'Devil' began drawing me in like a magnet. He seemed to have the ultimate power to get me to do anything he wanted. This power was my fearfulness and it was as though my soul was breaking.

"Fight him, fight him," I heard the voices in my head saying. *"You are strong, believe in yourself."*

All of a sudden I turned around and there was this magnificent light. It was Jesus standing there. The 'Devil' knew Jesus very well, and he said to him as he was laughing his head off,

"So you are here!"

Jesus said to the 'Devil,'

"Why do you want her? Leave her alone. She has come this far, deal with me not her."

I felt like I was a little child and that finally someone had come to rescue me.

This dark entity again laughed and said,

"She has passed the test, I will leave her alone."

"You can go now, you can go," Jesus said to me calmly.

I looked at him for reassurance and he said,

"You have passed your test; you will never come back here again."

My dreams have never taken me to that house again. Going face to face with the 'Devil' was the most unbelievable fear that one could ever imagine and I honestly didn't think I would get through it. I knew somewhere inside of me however if I didn't face it, I wouldn't be the person that I wanted to be. It was certainly the biggest challenge of my life. Light does actually break down the darkness.

"Imagine your negative thoughts or words are weeds and your positive thoughts or words are the rose. Which one do you want to nurture? Which one are you fertilising? Weeds will spread very quickly and will strangle and smother the rose. All the thoughts you have whether positive or negative are energy and create our reality. Be careful what you think, because what we give out we get back, not necessarily straight away, but it will come back to you. Why put your energy into something you don't want? This is the law of attraction. This is the law of the Universe,"

Beginning my Path in Mediumship

So many ideas were going around and around in my head as to how I was going to become a psychic medium in full time employment? Steve deserved answers and we both needed to know once my job finished I did have some other work to begin.

I had been massaging people for some time and when Spirit gave me a message for that person, I would say, "I have a feeling about this", and then proceed to tell them what Spirit had to say. I now realised Spirit wanted me to do more than this and be open about how I was able to communicate with the other side. There are still people who I massage who do not know that I am a psychic medium.

"What do you want me to do?" I desperately asked Spirit, "I just don't know where to start. Nobody knows I can do it and you're telling me all these people are going to come to see me!"

This really was proving to be a test of my trust and faith in Spirit.

"Make up some business cards with your name on it,"

Spirit told me. *"You will be giving readings to people from us here in Spirit to people who ask of your services. We will give people the information that they need to help them in their journeys on Earth. Each person that visits you for a reading will receive a small crystal in a velvet bag."*

It wasn't long before I found these two men working from out of their back shed who did digital cards. They had all this high tech machinery and within a week I had my new business cards. I had no job and to start the business I needed, two hundred and eighty dollars for the cards and twenty dollars to buy some crystals. So where would I get the three hundred dollars? I discovered at this point that Spirit never lets me down. That was on the Monday. My mother in law was now living in New Zealand, and she asked me if I would like to go to bingo with her that night.

I said, "I only have twenty dollars in my purse, so I will only be buying one card."

I got there and started to play with my one card. It got to the final round and the house had grown to three hundred dollars. The card had been terrible all night.

I should not have done this, but I said to Spirit,

"If you want me to work for you, and I said I would, please let me win this three hundred dollars so I can pay for my cards and some of the crystals!"

I started to do really well and I was waiting for one number to come up. I was going, 'Please, please, please, please' and then I heard,

"House!" I was so upset, some person had beaten me to it.

The woman who thought she had won called out her numbers, and the caller said,

"Sorry we haven't got that number," so he drew another number.

That number was 18, my number.

I jumped in the air as I said, "Thank you, thank you, thank you."

I got the money, and I did put it away as I promised. I went and collected my new printed cards. I then asked Spirit,

"What do I do now?"

"You put one card on a notice board," Spirit said.

I put it on the notice board at the local supermarket. I stood back and looked at it.

I said to Spirit, "Nobody is going to see that, or somebody will walk past and take it. Am I really only supposed to put one card up?"

"Trust," was all Spirit said.

Three days later, a woman phoned me up.

"Fiona here, I have your card in my hand."

It stopped me in my tracks. I felt nervous, and I thought I hope she doesn't ask me for a reading!

She said, "It's really weird, I am not Spiritual, but on Tuesday I was going to lunch. Usually I take a different route, and I don't walk past that notice board in the mall. But for some reason I did and I was drawn to your card. I took it off the notice board and put it in my pocket, and went back to work. I put it on my desk, and every morning in my head I heard a voice saying from I don't know where, 'Contact her, contact her.'"

So I said "Do you want a massage?"

"No," was her answer.

"Do you want a reading?"

"No," came the reply

"Do you want Reiki?"

"No," was her answer again. I was getting frustrated. What did this woman want?

"So what do you want?" I said, having run out of things that I could do.

Her reply blew me away, "I am a newspaper reporter and I want to do your life story."

She was to come on Tuesday at three o'clock. At 10 minutes to three, I got 'a call from the other side,' and they said,

"She is not coming till 10 minutes past three. She's late."

As soon as Spirit told me that the phone rang. I picked up the phone and said,

"Hi Fiona, you are running late. See you at 10 past three."

"Did the office phone you?" She asked.

"No Spirit told me."

This became the opening line of the feature article that Fiona wrote about me in the local paper. However there were no contact numbers in there and I was extremely disappointed when I saw this. I was sitting contemplating what I could do when the phone rang.

"My phone has been running red hot. Can I give your number out?" Was all I heard Fiona say. I should have known that Spirit was up there organising things for me.

That is how it all started. In the past years I have seen

hundreds of people and have not advertised myself. From this point my life changed. It became a very busy time.

"There is so much we want you to do," Spirit told me.

I was not ready for what was to happen next. Every situation I was in, Spirit was giving me information. I could not escape them. I would wake in the morning hearing them, and their voices in my head would be the last thing I heard at night as I went to sleep. Even my dream state was about receiving messages from them. In the end I had to say to them.

"Right, you can't give me information all the time as I am only human. I know you are there; I want you to be there, but only when I say 'come closer.'" I felt it was important for me to be in control of them.

I didn't feel or hear anything for days from them. I was totally lost.

I had this almighty panic come over me. They have gone, I have lost them. What am I going to do without them; they are such a big part of my life. I have taken Spirit for granted and this is the result.

I silently said, "What has happened? Where have you gone? Have I upset you?"

"Sorry, sorry, sorry," I said loudly.

"We are here but you haven't asked us for anything yet. You told us to stand by you and we have been here but you were blinded to us because of your own fears." Spirit was back!

When I am not working with clients, or I am having some time to myself, they stay quiet now except when it is urgent. Then they will tell me,

"We need to tell you this" and that is fine.

I have found when I don't listen to their advice it often goes wrong but instead of chastising me they ask, *"What have you learnt from that?"* I know it is to listen and to trust.

Spirit moved full steam ahead from this point.

"Guardian Angel Evenings," Spirit told me one day in the shower.

"What are Guardian Angel Evenings?" I enquired of Spirit.

"It is a way for you to grow confidence in your abilities and to get the word of Spirit out to many people in a fun and accessible way."

It wasn't long before the new 'Tupperware-like' parties had begun and I was inundated with requests to provide the amusement for 'girl's nights.' A person would book an evening with me, and invite five or so friends. I would go to their home, at about seven o'clock and I would go into a separate room, and each person would have a half-hour reading with me. A problem that arose was when the women weren't having the reading they were sitting in the lounge drinking. They would often get drunk and become quite rude.

Not everybody that was invited had knowledge of Spirit or really believed in psychic mediums. When I walked into people's homes I could pick up all the different energies that were going on in that home and I would be told whether they were going to accept me or not. Every evening provided at least one challenge. This proved to be really tiring, and some nights I would not get home to one o'clock and then I would have to be up the next morning to work. I was driving home one night and I was talking to Spirit and I said,

"I don't need to do this any more. This is not me. I am not a sideshow."

I realised again that Spirit had certainly given me another lesson and that I was able to return to my life's work focussing on doing my one-on-one readings, massage, Reiki, and some House Blessings. Steve built a room onto the side of our house so I could work out of there. I began to get very busy but every so often I would have my confidence knocked. For every very satisfied fifty people that would visit me, it would only take another one to completely throw me and make me question my abilities. I felt like I was on a roller coaster ride with my emotions at times.

"There are always going to be sceptics," Spirit said, *"who will test you until you totally believe in yourself. They are there to test you and strengthen your resolve of who you are. You will learn to be stronger."*

The doubting people did turn up. I was now aware however of the first clue as they would sit sideways and look at the wall and there would be no eye contact. Then the rudeness would begin and they would say things like "whatever, yeah whatever" or "you don't know what you are talking about." I would basically think they were saying, "You are telling me a load of rubbish." Many times when these people were coming to me by the end of the day I just cried and I would say to Spirit,

"I just can't keep on going on like this and being treated like this."

Spirit would say to me, *"You don't have to it's what you are accepting. You can accept them in the room or say, there is the door. You have the choice and it is in your power to do so, not theirs."*

Spirit telling me this, was a big lesson and I started putting it into practice. One day a man came in. He sat down and I started to talk to him. I could tell he was a non believer by his energy. He had completely shut himself off. I began to fumble and lose confidence in myself and then I heard Spirit say to me,

"You are going to do this whether he believes this or not."

I stopped the reading and said to him,

"Okay I am going to stop there. Your attitude is really rude, your body language is telling me you don't believe what I am saying and the way you are talking to me makes me give you two choices – you can either sit there and listen to what I have to say or there's the door. Which one would you like? Actually when it comes down to it, it's my choice as to whether I want you to sit there in my room and take my energy. So think about that!"

His mouth dropped and the little 'I' inside of me went Whoa! I was always taught never to answer anybody back or say what I thought and here I was doing all of that. So I said,

"Do you want to think about it because I know what I want right at this moment is for you to get up and leave me." I said, "Why did you come and see me if you are going to treat me like this?"

"I've got flatmates who came to see you and they said how really good you were and so I've come to test you," he replied beginning to look foolish.

I started to let fly, "I don't have to prove myself to you, I have done my apprenticeship. You are the one with the insecurities that you have to come here and prove something to yourself!"

This was not what he expected and he meekly began to apologise. We went on with the reading and he was amazed at what I could tell him. I am sure he went away with a whole new concept of Spirit and the learning that can be gained from the other side. As he left I said, assisted by Spirit,

"You walk on your own path and it is up to you whether you choose that path to be graced with light or tarnished with darkness."

"If you keep sending these people to me, I will not be doing this any longer."

"We are doing this to make you stronger."

"I have done it now, and I don't want anymore, thank you Spirit!"

Sceptics are few and far between now as I will not stand for it and I am more confident in myself and my abilities. I am always polite when putting my case across.

There are religious people who, when they hear what I do become very rude. Once two church people came to my door and they started talking to me and asked me what religion I was.

"I am Christian but I am also a Spiritual Medium."

You could see them back away.

"I know you won't believe in that, but you know what, you read all these things in the Bible yet you will judge me now but I don't judge you."

One said to me, "You are doing the Devil's work."

I said, "If I am hurting someone or causing harm to another person, yes then I would be working for the Devil, but I am not."

He said to me, "Then okay if Spirit is talking to you, what are they saying about me?"

This was my chance. I said, "You have a rash on your arm and it's just coming up."

"No I haven't," he said vehemently.

"Well if I am telling an untruth, and I am working with the Devil, roll your shirt sleeves up and let's have a look."

"I don't have to roll my sleeve up for you!" was his reply.

The other young man with him piped up and said, "You told me you had a rash on your arm this morning."

Embarrassed, the first young man said it was only slightly there. So I then was able to tell him he was allergic to seafood and he had had some mussels for dinner last night. He started to tell me I was wrong.

Again the second young man piped up and said,

"We were at those people's house last night and we did have mussels for dinner."

"What are you trying to prove?" was all I could say. "You need to look at yourself instead of trying to put me down?"

Well with that they walked away.

It always interests me that people have no understanding of what or how I work yet they are very quick to judge. Being a psychic medium does have its downside in social interactions and I can clear a room very quickly. Once I went with a friend to a fiftieth birthday party where there were very few people I knew. I sat down by this older lady who was very friendly and we chatted away until another woman came over who happened to be this woman's sister. As the conversation began to stall, the first lady said,

"So what do you do then?"

In the past I had a policy of not telling people, as I was embarrassed about my work and afraid of what people would think of me. With my increased abilities and success in my work I was now able to say,

"I am a Spiritual medium."

She had been leaning forward towards me. Well, literally her body straightened and she moved back in the chair. She looked at her sister and they began giving eye signals. The other sister said,

"Do you actually charge for this?"

"Sometimes I do and sometimes I don't," I said. "There are clients who are unable to pay and Spirit tells me this."

Her next statement bowled me over. "I think it is very bad for people like you to charge others."

"Do you go to work and do you get paid for it?" By this time I was getting infuriated.

"Of course I do," she smugly replied.

"Well I go to work as well and many people are very

happy to pay me for what I can share and assist them with."

At this point we each got up and found other more compatible people to chat with.

Spirit told me, *"To get on in this world with each other we need to learn respect for each other's beliefs and to not judge without any understanding of where people are at in their life. It is called tolerance."*

Some people do have a warped sense of what I do and how it should be done and will often air their misguided concept of me and my abilities such as the young man that said to me,

"I have been told that if you have a gift like yours it will be taken away from you if you charge people." I knew he was trying to take me for a fool and didn't want to pay.

So I said, "Well I have had it all my life and it hasn't been taken away from me yet. You know what; don't say things like that to me when you don't want to pay. Don't take me for a fool."

* * * *

"Finding direction in your lives by hearing the words from us here in Spirit, offering perspective on a situation through a psychic medium, or hearing the words from us yourself supports you on your journey through life. You choose your life and your situations for the tests that you will encounter to ensure that when it is time to pass over you have achieved all that you set out to do before you came to Earth.

During your lifetime there are things that will shackle you

and it is up to you as to how you move through these periods. Often when encountering a test you are unable to see where you are supposed to be or why this is happening. It's like you're thrown into a river and the undercurrent is going so fast that are you not sure where you are going.

Knowing that somewhere there is a log that you could hold on to or that you will be steered over to the side supports you on your journeys. The rapids of your life make you flow to the point where you know not where you are going but take the ride and know that you will be safe."

Being confident to visit a psychic medium depends on each individual as to whether they believe that there is a higher force working behind the scenes in all of our lives or not. By understanding and trusting this belief it will allow Spirit to come in and guide each one of us. The turbulence that we all experience in life can be eased. As we move into this age of illumination, more and more people are choosing to visit Psychic Mediums as they look for insightful direction. People are becoming more aware that there is another side to our existence, that when you die you don't actually die. This is why the term passing over is used. Once when Spirit heard a journalist use the word death in the question, they said to me,

"That's a dirty word. To us it is like those ghastly swear words that are used on your Earth."

My goal for each person who visits me is that they will gain some clarity of past, present and sometimes future situations. From this they will be able to appreciate that all their experiences have and will make them who they are today. Being able to move on in a positive way in their lives is my overriding aim for each client.

People look at me and think I am a medium all the time, but I still have fears and doubts just like everybody else. Every day, until recently, I have fought my feelings of the impossibility of what I am doing. Deep down inside I have still been carrying the remnants of all the misguided opinions I received from my family all those years before. By keeping myself balanced and trying not to overwork I can ensure that these unwelcome insecure beliefs do not resurface again. I have had readings from other mediums, and other mediums visit me. Even though I have a wonderful connection with Spirit, I find a need for confirmation or clarification in my life. At times, I feel overwhelmed that I can actually contact the other side and need reassurance from outside sources.

Someone once said to me,

"Why would you go and see another medium when you are one yourself?"

In my head I asked Spirit, "Why do I do that sometimes?" The answer came back,

"Does a dentist drill his own teeth?"

My client and I laughed as we heard the answer from Spirit but it certainly did give us the answer we could understand.

My Guides

Everybody has specific ways of contacting and gaining guidance from Spirit. For me, I have been blessed with the abilities of clairvoyance (seeing Spirit), clairaudience (hearing Spirit), and clairsentience (feeling Spirit). The more I work with Spirit the more my abilities have developed and have become stronger. During a reading each of these abilities are available to me and Spirit comes in, in the way that is most appropriate for the client. The room can be overflowing with Spirit at times.

There are the angels, mine and the clients as well as the universal angels, my guides, passed loved ones of the client, and the clients guides, so it can be extremely busy. They are intermixing and providing information all the time. When I become inundated I have to ask them all to stop as it is too much. Our family members that have passed over still have an opinion. One young woman who came to me for a reading was shocked when a loved one said,

"We are not so keen on your new partner."

"Don't they like him?" she asked thinking that what comes from the other side is what we must follow.

Knowing the angels come through on a different level and offer a different unbiased and deeper point of view, I asked them.

"He is fine but there are areas that you need to look at."

Spirit is not there to upset anyone. It is all about what you need to hear to improve your life.

"Understand, guides are like teachers." Spirit told me. *"Each guide works at a different level and will bring in increasing abilities for you to work with. It is like your education system. You begin at kindergarten and you have teachers that teach you at that level. You progress up through the system learning at the appropriate level. Some will go on to University and others will not. So it is with the Spirit world. Your guides that vibrate with your level of energy will guide you on the rung of the ladder you have attained and will prepare you to go higher. Each rung up moves you into a new department and new guides will come in. Spirit has many levels as to how you will work with them. With each new level you will be tested."*

Unlike the school system, when working with Spirit it is not an automatic move up the ladder. It may take years to go up a rung and receive a new 'teacher'. Since I made the commitment of working with Spirit, I now recognise when a new guide is coming in and that I am going up another level. Initially I become extremely disorientated as my energy body alters so I can move up into their higher energy vibration. I will appear lost and disorganised and then it's WOW and things start to change with the increase in the energy level. It is a higher consciousness who chooses who will be our guides.

Our personal guides are souls who have passed over after obtaining many life lessons on Earth and now no longer need to reincarnate. All the learning that they have had throughout their lives is now used for the betterment of mankind. For me this is my last life time here as I will be moving into being a Spiritual guide or teacher for people back on Earth.

At present I have three personal guides who also come through to assist me. They are like my managers, keeping me in line and offering insight. One is an older lady called Margaret, who is English and very prim and proper. Margaret chose me to work with and keeps me on track in my readings. Often she says to me,

"Come on, come on, they are not here to listen to that. You can talk later. This person is here to have a reading."

Margaret spoke to me while being interviewed for this book and told me a bit more about her life. On listening to the recordings we actually heard Margaret talking before I brought the information through. A number of clients have reported they hear the guides uttering when they replay the tape made from their reading with me. Margaret says,

"I have not long passed. I was born in 1920 and I passed at sixty-seven. I was a medium and I belonged to a Spiritualist church in England. I did do some platform work but the committee of the church I was with were stuck in their ways unable to look outside the square at times. This limited my growth. Spirit would give me direction on where the church could go but this was not taken up as I was seen as going way beyond their realm of awareness.

For you though, all of us here in Spirit are guiding and encouraging you to move beyond what you ever thought you were capable of achieving. You are outgrowing me as you are now moving ahead of what I achieved as a medium. A higher

level guide will be coming into your energy vibration to advance you further. I will move on to assisting others in their psychic abilities. Your Grandmother Florence tells me how very proud she is of what you are achieving. Remember to pace yourself as you go forward in this earthly existence. Always know that Spirit is sorting everything out and the way is being cleared for all to happen in your life."

I felt sad with the thought of Margaret going. She is like a grandmother to me and is always nurturing me just as Florence did.

A Chinese doctor from the time of the Ming Dynasty is my second guide. His hair is long and plaited and he has a long moustache. He is only small, very funny and wears the most beautiful red and gold robes. When he first appeared in my readings I had a female client who wasn't feeling well. Her first question to me was if I could ask the other side what was the matter with her. All of a sudden the Chinese doctor was there and I said,

"I have a man here and he tells me he is my new guide."

He came in so strong and I started talking to the client in a Chinese accent. We laughed and he laughed along with us and then I started telling her all these things. He will appear only when I ask for assistance when people need to know about their health from a deeper perspective than the answers the other guides are giving me. He moves around the client, scanning their body and then will tell me what is going on for them.

Many people who do come to me know there is something not right with them and unfortunately they haven't got the answers from the medical profession. I am not a medical physician and when this situation does arise in a reading and the possibility of what it is does come through I always tell people to have it checked out by their own doctor. Passed loved ones do not always have the medical experience to assist Doctor Ming but will still often give an opinion. At times I have to ask the room full of Spirit to quieten down and let the job be done by those with the greatest knowledge of the problem. When I am giving a healing it is about various energies that all have different abilities working through me for that person.

'Doctor Ming' also assists me with my health.

"He told me that I have glandular fever and he said for me to come and see you," I said to my doctor pointing to the ceiling.

The doctor perched on the end of his seat and said,

"Who told you?"

"You have got to change what you have just said," Spirit quickly jumped in.

My mind was racing as the doctor peered over the top of his glasses at me.

"You hear voices?"

"He thinks you are a schizophrenic. You need to do something about this now!" Spirit instructed me.

"No I had a dream." I am sure the doctor didn't believe me so after receiving my prescription I hurriedly left, never returning to that doctor again. I now have a doctor who listens and trusts what I tell her.

As I drove home Spirit said to me,

"Hearing voices that may want you to harm yourself or

someone else and hearing the word of Spirit is completely different. Spirit only brings loving energy and information through and you know you are loved no matter what. You can shut us off, whereas schizophrenics can never do that unless they take medication."

After this experience I always impress on clients that when it is recommended to see a doctor that they do not say how they heard this. Unfortunately not everyone heeds my warning.

"Your energy is very, very low." I told a client, "You are very ill."

"This woman has Mercury poisoning," 'Doctor Ming' said very clearly and loudly.

"You have mercury poisoning and you need to see a doctor about it very soon. Please do not tell your doctor that you have received a psychic message about your health as generally they are not in tune to this."

The woman promptly went to the doctor and said she had mercury poisoning as she had been told by a psychic medium. His comment was 'a load of rubbish and don't listen to this so called psychic person. There is nothing physically the matter with you. It is all in your head. After a number of visits to him repeatedly asking for help he sent her to the psychiatric unit at the hospital.

After a year the woman returned to me and I couldn't believe the change in her. Her hands were crippled and bent up and she had lost so much weight through the daily vomiting and diarrhoea. She had a constant headache. Her business as a hairdresser had gone as it was impossible to hold the scissors or a brush. I knew she was desperate but she seemed to be losing her will.

"It is not in your mind, it is in your body," I reassured her.

"She is very close to passing over. This woman needs a test for mercury poisoning." Spirit told me of a place I had never heard of that she was to go to.

I then literally saw this needle going into her arm and Spirit told me,

"She will receive a very large dose of concentrated Vitamin C."

"What is Vitamin C for?" I asked Spirit.

"It attaches to the mercury molecules like a magnet, and then the body flushes it out through the urine."

I relayed this to the woman, but fear came over her as she had no money or job to pay for this treatment.

She decided to ask her sister. I was praying for it to be right as she was going to spend a lot of money for these tests. She got back in contact with me after she found the place and had the test results back. The clinic needed to see her urgently as it was one of the highest readings for mercury poisoning the clinic had ever seen. They told her they would be injecting her with vitamin C to clear it from her body. She had acquired all this mercury through the hair product that she had used over the years. Her health rapidly improved after this and recently I saw that she had opened another hair salon.

Clients also come to me for readings that have very specialised medical conditions. My Chinese doctor guide does not always have the specialised experience or knowledge to be able to comment on the direction the person needs to take towards well health. This is when the many passed over people with wonderful talents and abilities gained from their time on earth and extended on the other side can come in and assist. They are waiting to be asked. When the situation arises I very quickly say to all Spirit,

"Please come in, the most appropriate medical specialist that can assist this person."

You can use this technique in all areas of your life from asking for passed over motor mechanics to tell you about your car, to sitting exams and calling in knowledgeable people in that area. My friend's children use this technique with their school and university exams and assignments and it has never let them down yet.

A lady came to me and whatever else was going on in her life it was her health that was of concern. As soon as 'Doctor Ming' came in, he told me I needed to ask a specialist to come in.

"Spirit is telling me you need an operation on your spine. You are not sure which way to go. I know this will sound strange but I am going to call in one of the top orthopaedic surgeons."

So I calmly said,

"Right everyone I am looking for a top orthopaedic surgeon over there."

She was looking at me as though I was crazy and had definitely lost my marbles.

Spirit brings through who they feel would best suit the client and who they would trust and respond to.

The Harley Street surgeon, who came in dressed in his

pin stripe suit, speaking with most perfect English accent and using exactly the right medical terms was perfect for this woman.

The next thing I knew I began drawing the spine. The surgeon was telling me,

"Part of her spine is starting to crumble and collapse."

I pointed to the picture of the spine I had now drawn and said right here pointing to an exact spot.

"That is right!" she exclaimed.

"This woman has two options here. The spine can be fused with a steel rod and she will not be able to bend over or there is new technology now where there are plastic disks that can be inserted to replace the deteriorating ones. Go to your consultant and say you will go with the plastic disk option. Do you want to ask me anything?"

"Could you understand all of that?" I said

The story then came out of how she had been to two orthopaedic surgeons and one said that a steel rod in the back was an option and the other surgeon had told her about the new plastic inserts. She had to make a decision that week and now she had the guidance to assist her with the decision.

"Amazing," was all she could say.

My third guide is my main guide. He is very powerful and very protective of me. When I am feeling a little afraid when I know a client is coming in who is going to test me and I need to be assertive, I will feel his powerful energy come in. It lifts me. I sit up and I start talking with a very strong manner. He is extremely positive and doesn't stand for anything.

"What is your name?" I asked this guide as I felt I needed a more personal connection. This main guide said to me,

"What's in a name? It's not about a name it's about why I am here to work with you."

His role is to oversee me. To keep things and myself grounded by ensuring I continue to believe in myself. He works on a very different vibration and he brings in the masculine energy which gives my life balance. He has been with me for about four years.

For a short while I had a guide who was exceedingly bossy. I wasn't allowed to laugh or joke. One night while giving a talk he came in and started telling me off. I told the audience that my guide had come in and what he was saying to me. I wasn't making a joke out of it, it's just who I am. When I was driving home afterwards, he started saying to me,

"How dare you do that! How dare you make a joke of me!"

He would've picked up the annoyance in my voice when I said,

"Well if you don't like it, go and find some one else. I didn't ask you to be my guide."

"I will," he abruptly said and I never had him back again. We do have choices about our guides and this one just didn't work out for either of us.

Spirit will take me to wherever they want me to go as I am an instrument for them to bring their communication through. An antenna is how I like to see it. When I was a child and passed loved ones and people who weren't even related appeared, I would literally see them in solid form as the person they were on Earth. There was always a mist around them. The best way to describe it is if you take a photograph using the older type camera and you haven't wound it around, you get an overlap.

As I have become more experienced with the other side, I now usually see them only as mist. I know and accept that they are there so Spirit does not need to appear in such a solid form. If the client requires proof of who is coming through from the other side the solid form may appear so I can describe the passed loved one. I can feel them as well and run my hands around the perimeter of their energy bodies to describe height and shape.

Impressing on the client that the term passing over is more applicable than the term dying when our physical life ends is important so they can understand life goes on in another dimension. Many people ask how the millions of people that die everyday can fit on the other side. My answer is that we are just in an energy form that is able to shift and therefore move through a 'doorway' to an area surrounding Earth that some call heaven.

Passed loved ones still have their personality from their earth lifetime as it is imprinted on them. At times with clients there is much hilarity when the individuality of the passed over person comes through and their characteristics used to be like this and their grandma used to be like that. Spirit does like us to laugh.

Yes it is serious when someone passes over but during the reading something will come through that will make them laugh, and this is something they can take away with them.

Passed loved ones will also tell the client what they think of their new partner, or their new house or their new job. I do cry with people as well as I feel the pain they are going through, but at the end of the day I let it go as it doesn't belong to me. I have to be in control at all times as the clients need this to feel safe.

How the person passed is always given to me as well. Sometimes I get their name, sometimes I don't. I asked Spirit one day,

"Why is it that sometimes I get the person's name and sometimes I don't?"

"It depends how high the antenna is that day. Some people on the other side have a weaker link than others and they need to learn how to communicate from their new position. There will always be some coming in stronger than others.

Because someone gets more names than another person, does not make them a better psychic. Each of you who work with Spirit is blessed with different abilities. Some see auras, some astral travel, some channel through writings, some will see Spirit in depth, some will hear Spirit out loud and some through their Spiritual ears will receive the words or voices within their mind.

Every person born to this Earth has a sixth sense or psychic abilities but they are all at different levels. It is a bit like with musical ability, some will play like Mozart and others will stick with basic 'chopsticks' and so it is with Spiritual development."

Spirit can tell people what they are here to learn on earth such as patience, perseverance, trust, kindness and their life experiences will reflect this. The so-called good and the bad events of a person's life can come through with the passed person in the reading. They show me how it used to be and it is important to understand that if there had been intolerable situations on earth it is no longer like this in Spirit. Anything horrible that may have happened on the earth plane with the passed over person and the client, the hostility and bitterness that may have been there is not brought through.

Passed loved ones on the other side do have choices, just as we do on earth. They can decide whether they come through in a reading or not. Sometimes the passed over person has difficulty getting across what they have done, or what has been done to them and they hold on to it. Healing on the other side can take a long time and generally a passed over person who has not healed sufficiently will not make their presence felt in the reading. When my mother comes through, now that she has healed there is only forgiveness in each of our souls. The other side is all about peace and harmony but for some it takes longer to achieve this.

Other Realms of Guidance

Angels have been with me since I was a young child when I would see them as beautiful gentle energies that were either male or female. When we are children we are very open and receptive to the Angel energy as we don't have all the responsibilities, cares and worries that we have as adults. The angels can take on the recognised picture book form of celestial beings with wings on their backs so we know they are there. I still cherish the thought of what I was told as a young child that our shoulder blades are where our wings have been clipped.

I, at times would tell my family that I saw angels hoping they would listen and believe me. My mother, who never shared personal things with me, for whatever reason told me in a weak moment that she saw an angel. She said she was a little girl, it was dark, she was in her bedroom, she was upset and she was crying. In the corner of the room this magnificent light lit the whole room up. This was the only time she ever spoke of anything Spiritual. It was confirmation for me, that what I was seeing was real and I hung onto this story to keep on believing.

Angels are what you perceive them to be. Many adults do see them but do not recognise what they are seeing. That flash of light out of that corner of the eye is often an angel.

The angels now, when I am doing a reading come in as vibrations of light. I see their outline enter the room, I have the feelings of them in my third eye and I am able to hear and converse with them in my mind. The angels are always there for guidance and strength and they are asking each one of us now to begin connecting with their realm.

Every single soul at birth is assigned at least one angel until you pass over and then your angels are assigned to another soul. There is no retirement in the angelic world. They are there to guide, support and protect us. When people are having the reading I am able to see the angels surrounding them and this tells me a lot about the person's life mission. The most I have ever seen is nine around one lady who was heavily involved in doing charity work.

"The angels stand by your side and act as your co-workers but you are their managers," was how Spirit described them.

It is very effortless to begin working with the angels and to quickly see the results. For years I have called in my 'parking angels' when looking for a car space. I visualise where I am going and then ask the angels to find the appropriate park. It will always be there. Once when I had to drive around the block two times and then found the original space I visualised, Spirit said to me,

"This was a lesson for you to understand that at times assistance from the angels is not always instant. In life for

everything to be in place you may have to wait longer from the time of asking. It's about learning patience, trust and knowing that the angels will organise things if it is for your soul's growth. The angels will not do anything that will harm another's soul or put you in a position that is not right for you to do that particular thing.

We understand you will not wait six months for a parking space. If a person is looking for a house or is going to meet that someone special, that house that is right for them may not be on the market yet or the person may not even be in the country yet. Maybe you are going after a job and you really want it and you don't get it. It's not because you weren't capable but there is something better around the corner or perhaps your life is to go in another direction. If it is not meant to be, the angels will stop working or not even commence on it for you to get the thing that you are asking for."

The angels have been very busy in my life and have always been there for me when I have asked. When we returned from England we lived in a rented house in a farming area. One morning I was late for work and I hurried to get into my car and rush off. In the country there are no street lights, so it was extremely dark. At the end of the long road and over the rise was the village. Unbeknown to me there had been a water main burst in the village and my little yellow Honda Civic was being driven rather fast. I could hear the angels saying,

"You've got to slow down, now. You've got to slow down!"

As I got to the petrol station—on the corner, there was apparently very deep water. I could see people on the side of the road with lights waving me down to slow down and stop. I hit the water and it spun my car round. My whole life was flashing in front of me. It was very fast-moving. I had forgotten to put my seatbelt on as I was in such a hurry. My ribs were hitting the steering wheel; my head was hitting the window. The impact just took me and spun me around.

"Help me, help me!"

Again I heard the angels, saying they were protecting me.

"It is all right, you'll make this."

I came to a stop, six inches from the petrol tank. I opened the door of the car, and all the water came rushing in. I injured my hips, my neck had whiplash, and there was a large cut on my leg. When water gets in your brakes you are at the mercy of the incident.

The angels remind us,

"We all have free will and to gain their assistance we only need to ask."

There are tiers of angels besides our personal angels, all working to assist us. The most powerful group are the Archangels, each having a specific role and each able to assist everyone at the same time. Archangel Michael is often around me in my personal life and in the readings giving strength and protection. I know when he is there as I see a purple mist appear and I strongly feel his presence. Archangel Raphael will come in, in healing sessions, Archangel Gabriel for creative assistance and Archangel Uriel for dealing with emotions. There are many more Archangels so just call when you need them to be around you.

The Ascended Masters are another form of Spirit that also appear to me in the readings and in my life. This group contain people such as Mother Mary, Buddha, and others who have lived exceptional lives on this Earth and have now passed. They return in Spirit to teach us some of the wisdom of life. Jesus is one such Ascended Master and has appeared to me a number of times in critical situations for myself and also for clients.

A very Spiritual and intelligent lady from India came to see me for healing. She was alone and had come to New Zealand as she had been shunned by her family for having a child out of wedlock. The boy was now seven. I was giving her Reiki and I was positioned at her head. There down towards her feet Jesus appeared. He said to me,

"You must tell this woman what I am to show you."

I then saw her attempting to commit suicide. She was also taking her child with her.

"You must tell her this must not be done, things will change."

She came out of that Reiki session and I said to her,

"You might not understand this. I just saw Jesus standing at the bottom of the bed by your feet and he said to me that you must not attempt to take your own or your son's life."

She looked at me in such shock and said,

"How dare you say that to me!"

I continued,

"You mustn't. Things will work out you mustn't do this. You must trust that all will be well it will be okay."

She seemed very angry with me but still made another appointment the following week.

Two days later while I was at home on Friday night I kept seeing this woman in my head. I was getting ready to go out when the phone rang and I heard her say,

"A voice in my head keeps on telling me to phone you. I can't take it any more. I am going to give myself and my son an overdose."

"Jesus told you not to do this. I know you saw him at the end of the bed as well. Why were you so angry with me when I told this to you?"

She broke down.

"Because I knew it was true and I couldn't admit it to you."

"Please don't do this. You'll make it through this."

"I have prepared my son now."

"What do you mean?"

"I have settled him down and told him we are both going to go to sleep and not to be afraid."

I continued to reason with her for a long time and when she finally realised that she was doing the wrong thing I said to her,

"You have to undo what you have just said to your son."

I prayed for her that night and thank the Universe she is still around.

Most people on this earth have heard of Jesus and know of the amazing work and healing that he did. He was able to uplift all. Jesus is such a powerful Ascended Master and comes into my readings for my strength and to give that strength to others. He does come in at our times of need. Whenever Jesus does appear it often moves me to tears as I am so overwhelmed by his presence. A number of my clients have also seen him when he appears in their healing. He often stands at the end of the bed holding a person's feet. When we say, "Oh my God" we are actually calling on the highest of energies.

Every day life as a Psychic Medium

Every day when I go to work I have absolutely no idea how the day will unfold. Since appearing in the television series *Sensing Murder*, where Psychic Mediums help investigate unsolved murder cases, there has been quite a change in the type of client who visit me. I now tend to get a lot more people who are dealing with uncertainty such as suicide, car accidents, drowning and murder. It is a big change from people asking if they should buy a new fridge or such like, as did happen often in the past. I am now prepared for anything and I have faith I can deal with all situations.

Having a reading helps the client to gain an understanding as to what has happened to their loved one. This can be quite difficult for me and draining, as I at times will endure what has happened to the person who passed, especially if it is a sudden passing. I will see, feel and hear it all, as I relive it.

Recently, a person came through who had taken their life by hanging. I began to feel the ropes around my neck, slowly, choking the air out of me. My voice had nearly gone and my eyes were watering. The client wondered what was going on. In my head I said to Spirit,

"Ask her loved one to back away from me so I can catch my breath."

I could tell her exactly how their loved one committed suicide. I was also able to tell this person that her own son had thought about doing this and the loved one wanted her son to know that he was not wanted over on the other side.

The beauty of the reading was that this woman was then able to go home and tell her son what I had told her and that I would like to see him. I did see him and he has been able to work through his depression with insight from the other side. Spirit talks about the passing and then moves on to helping the living.

When people sit in front of me for the reading, some of them are a bit overwhelmed as to what they are going to be told. People coming for their first reading will often say to me to ease their nervousness,

"I don't know why I am here?"

"Spirit has guided you here, so there has to be a reason. Relax and we will look at what is coming up for you," I say comfortingly.

"Besides passed over loved ones or friends we will work with your angels and your specific guides. Even if you do not know anyone who has passed over there are past entities that will come through. A reading is not always about contacting somebody that you knew who passed over."

Each session is begun with a prayer or invocation to ask Spirit to come through and also to align the energies of the client with Spirit. It is Spirit doing the work not me. The prayer also assists with easing the client into quietening and focusing their mind. I incorporate their name in the prayer to personalise it. I say to the client

"If you don't mind, I am going to say a prayer."

It doesn't matter what religion or beliefs that my clients have, they all close their eyes. Only a couple of times in all the years that I have been working has anyone ever said they were against a prayer being said. I believe a prayer is critical to my work so I just say,

"Well that's okay" and I get on with it. It's the way I work as I believe Spirit guides them to me when they are ready. All religions, Hindus, Muslims, Catholics, Protestants, Christians, Orthodox Jews, and Atheists come for readings.

When a person sits down I ask them not to say anything as I don't want to be influenced by them. The reading begins by looking at the person's aura and drawing and discussing the colours that I see around each person. New clients are sometimes a bit tentative as they think I can read their minds. I don't. I see the mind of people as having a barbed wire electric fence around it and it is private to that person. All the information that comes to me, comes from Spirit on the other side. When I relay a message people will now and then say,

"I was only thinking about that the other day. Are you reading my mind?"

People can become frightened by my abilities and how all this information can be received and given initially.

I am able to connect to people's energy, living and passed and also able to gather information through a photo of someone, or items such as their ring, watch, or piece of jewellery. Then I will move on to automatic writing or give the messages by speaking the channelled information through as Spirit gives it to me. The information can come incredibly fast. I don't even know where I am going, or what I am writing or saying. Sometimes I have to recap, and I say to the client,

"Did I say....?" And they look at me a bit strangely, like don't you know what you're saying?

Whatever Spirit wants me to talk about, it will come out. With some clients who are nervous about the reading or require proof that I am real, Spirit will chat away and will tell the person about the new carpet, what colour they painted their house, or about the new car. Then they will move on to the most important things that are going on for that person at that time. As soon as the client sits down Spirit is there and as soon as the person has gone Spirit associated with that person have also gone.

Spirit has been known to appear to me before the client arrives as they are so eager to make contact. I was in the kitchen next to my office one day, talking to a friend and all of a sudden, a man in Spirit appeared in the doorway. He was dressed in an air force uniform. I asked him what he wanted.

"I am waiting for your next person," he excitedly told me.

"Come back in half an hour and then I will be ready for you. I am having my lunch."

When the client did arrive, she sat down and I started talking to her,

"He is back. There is a man here. He is dressed in an air force uniform and you have the photo of him with you."

She took a photo she had brought out of her handbag and there was the picture of the man I was seeing in his air force uniform.

"He's been here some time waiting for you to arrive," I told her.

It was her father, who had been a fighter pilot in the war.

"The speed at which a passed loved one comes through depends on the person that has passed," Spirit said to me. *"Just like on Earth some people have that urge to get up and do things and others sit back and wait."*

When people first pass over its like they have gone to a foreign country and they are not sure how everything works on the other side. When they finally discover that they can contact their loved ones or someone that can help them tell their story back on earth they go looking for the connection. They find a 'phone box' that is connected to the switchboard and on the other end of the line is the psychic medium or someone who is capable of speaking their language. I am Spirit World's switchboard operator.

I also have to be able to decipher what the loved one is saying. They will give me symbols such as the man who came through and was putting a large marshmallow on the table before throwing it away. He was after the term 'mellowed out,' as this was a term he and his wife had used before he passed.

Another time I kept on seeing a red door and I was thinking the client had a red door in her house. All of a sudden Spirit let me know it was perfume and this woman's mother was telling her she liked her new brand of perfume, which was exactly the new perfume she had bought that week.

Passed loved ones know when a person is coming for a reading. A thought form moves very quickly and Spirit will do amazing things to get their loved ones in to see me. Even though I am so booked up there will be a cancellation or something will happen. There is no such thing as coincidence.

My receptionist had booked this person in twice by mistake. She didn't realise and when the person was rung for the reminder of the appointment for the next day he said,

"I have already been but my mother is desperate for an appointment and could she please have this one?"

Somehow she was guided to let the mother have the appointment, even though we do have a strict list. The mother had never heard of me, but as soon as she sat down I said,

"You are supposed to be here. There is a man here."

I described him and she brought a photo out.

"That's him," I said, "He's your brother, (I gave the name) who has recently drowned and everyone is saying he has taken his life. He is here to tell you that he didn't take his life."

The inquest was going to be held and he wanted to tell the truth.

Often, I am the first person that the past loved one can communicate with on earth so sometimes the passed loved ones do not want the reading to finish. Spirit learns to understand that they can not come into other people's readings. I have to have rules and regulations when I am working.

My grandfather came in once. I said to the client "can you just wait a minute while I tell my granddad to go away for now and come back in an hour."

A passed loved one came through on one occasion and he just stood there not saying anything. It was the client's father who had passed within the past few months. I said to him out loud,

"You have to talk to me because that is what I do and if you don't talk to me I can't do my job. You will have to let somebody else come through."

The woman client laughed, "My father didn't believe in clairvoyance when he was alive."

Past Lives

Spirit will look at the past of the person if they seem to be stuck in that space. Seeing who the person was and how they had lived in their past lives also adds information for the reading. The person in the reading sitting in front of me, just changes and their past life unfolds in front of me. It is a bit like I am watching a television screen. I will be sitting at my desk in my office when all of a sudden I will be transported to see a past lifetime that has significance so the client can understand what the issues are for their soul development. I have done this for myself also.

Whenever I saw a film on television to do with slavery I would be fascinated but would also become really upset because of the way they were treated. It was something inside of me that actually knew what they were going through. When I got older I began doing a meditation on this and I asked Spirit to show me the connections of the energies of me feeling this way with coloured people.

I was a boy about ten years of age and I was living on the coast of Africa and saw myself out playing when I saw the boats coming in. At the time I didn't know what they were as I had never seen anything like this before.

The next thing there were these men coming ashore and I knew instinctively something wasn't right. I started to run to my village to tell the others that strange looking people were coming. I was caught as were many of the other villagers. I could hear the women and other children screaming as we were all taken to the boat.

We were shackled to wooden slats below the deck on three layers. I was on the bottom layer and I had to endure the excrement of those above. I can still smell it now - it makes me want to vomit. Every so often buckets full of sea water were thrown over us to keep us clean. There were many of us and we were fed only bread and water, many were vomiting and a number died. I saw what happened when someone died. They would be cut at the ankles and wrists to free their bodies from the shackles and then disposed of overboard. The ones who survived and made it to the new country had a choker chain put around their necks. Before someone bought us we were carefully looked over from head to foot and even in our mouths. I was bought by a well-to-do businessman but was treated like a dog. He would pull me along by my neck chain and laugh as he did this.

When I was at school in Birmingham we visited a place in London that held all the records of people. On the wall was a painting of a man with the name Joseph Bagley who had owned a cotton plantation and had many slaves in America. Spirit told me he was a grandfather of mine many generations removed. On returning home when I excitedly told my father he would have none of it.

The legacy of my ancestry was born out further when I was twenty one and I went into the hospital to have my wisdom teeth removed. Inside my mouth, the dentist commented to me that I have a bone that protrudes and could tell me that you only find this in black Africans. Again, a few years ago while visiting an Iridologist she could tell me I had pure brown eyes with no blue in the background. Your ancestry, she told me had to be black African, Indian or Islander. I have obviously reincarnated into the same family that I have experienced in other lifetimes.

Another significant life time came out in me when I was a child. We had a gas cooker and sometimes the pilot light would go out and I would turn the gas on and just stand there actually frozen by it. In meditation I saw myself in the most recent past life before I was born.

I was a very well educated person – a professor of philosophy and I was in a concentration camp writing in a journal hoping that someday somebody would find it and discover something of what it was like to live this way. Next I saw a young guard come to get me and as he did he apologised as to what he had to do.

I was lead up the steps of a building with so many other people and I was put in the gas chamber. That guard has reincarnated to this earth at this time and happens to be a person whom I have met recently during a reading. Releasing these feelings for this woman through acknowledgement of what had happened certainly has helped both of us.

Jesus came to me and reminded me as he has done

many times, in many situations, with the same words,
"Forgive them, for they know not what they do.'

In recent times a woman came to me and I said to her,
"I can see you in a past life. You are a little girl about three or four, and you are out on the plains of Africa. You are with your parents and you have bare feet as you run through the tall grass. You look so happy with your blue eyes and fair hair. You were not a missionary family but rather a family looking for new adventures. All of a sudden I see you fall and you have gone. I can still hear your mother and father in the background and see your house.

"But why have you died? Show me why Spirit?"

"There is this big spider walking away from you. The venom worked on you very quickly as you are so little. I can still see your mother looking for you in the long grass. You have two marks on one of your feet now. Two prongs."

As she was taking her shoes off, she said,

"I am petrified of spiders." On her foot were two prong marks. She had bought these through from a previous life.

Often we don't know where fears and phobias we have, have come from. They can be brought back into this present lifetime from our previous existences. I work with people in therapy to look at these to see which past life it has come from and then we work on healing to let go of that memory. We also have talents and abilities that come through from past lives as well and this can assist the client in finding their true purpose in this lifetime.

Of late this ability of 'television viewing' enables me to go to someone's house or into a situation and I can then describe it to the client. This only comes in when I am doing a reading. Spirit comments on many things and takes me to many places. I cannot guess the things that come through and I can not guess the things that I am talking about.

Healing Touch

Some people come to me who are terminally ill and are looking for guidance, healing, how can they live the last part of their life and if and when they pass over what will it be like. Spirit never tells me when a person is going to pass over. The first time someone was coming to me for this direction, I wondered how I was going to approach it. I was quite frightened. Spirit said to me,

"The first thing you are going to say to them is 'Do you want to live?' There will be a yes or no."

I have continued to use this approach and when I say that to people they look at me and some will say "yes of course I do." Then Spirit works on that as we know the mind can help heal the body. When the person lingers over the question of their mortality and they think and pause, they often say "I am not sure." Spirit then takes a different approach. Spirit will ask me to ask,

"If you were to pass over to the other side tomorrow and someone over there said to you 'So if you had your life again, what would you like to have done or achieved.' What is your answer? It's still not too late to do these things."

Spirit looks at it this way. If you haven't the will to live then nothing that they are going to say will help. I, in union with Spirit will talk to them about me going to the other side and what it is like over there. I used to be embarrassed telling people how I had visited there when I tried to commit suicide, but I am over that now so I can share this experience. If my knowledge can help one person then I will tell the world. I talk to people about who they are going to meet, what its like, and then I say,

"You are going home. We are only visiting here; this is not our true home. You are going to see all your loved ones. You will meet people who you had a grudge against but over there you can sort it out. There's no point in carrying any extra luggage that you don't want over on the other side."

Spirit always uses great analogies.

"Its like you're going on holiday and you are packing all these clothes and you know you are never going to wear them. We only take what we need to the other side."

So any follow-up session is about how they are living each moment, each day and each month or year of their lives.

"Are you Sue Nicholson who does healing?" I was asked in the street one day by a lady.

"I have a desperately ill son who has leukaemia and he doesn't have long to live. The treatment he is having is making him very ill and they don't know if he will survive. Would you be able to see him?"

"We have guided this woman to meet you and so it will be fine to go ahead with her request," they assured me before I answered.

"Yes I will see your son and we will do our best to get him through this. If it is his time however there is nothing I can do."

"Could I sit in on the session with him?"

"That would be alright," I said, "As long as you only hold positive thoughts in your mind and do not allow any thoughts of him passing. You have to see him healthy and well and you have to send that out. I do not want any tears or any sadness. We have to work together and have that collective energy. The higher the positive power in the room then the higher the power that will flow through."

I managed to fit him in the next day. He was a young man of only twenty and he was very frightened. He had been having chemotherapy administered through his neck. I laid him on the bed and asked him to shut his eyes.

"Do you want to live?" was my first question.

He quickly replied, "Yes I do, I don't want to die."

I said a prayer and asked all the healing angels and everyone on the other side to help me. I placed my hands on him and began to work. He had a very dark energy within him. Illness is a deep dark dense energy.

When we had finished I asked him if he was okay.

All he could say was, "I didn't feel anything I only saw blackness."

"That's okay we will break through that," I said.

At the conclusion of the second session four days later he said,

"I saw this pin hole of light, just like a flicker of a match. I looked at it and focused on it. The rest was black."

"At least we have the light coming through now." I said.

Then at the end of the third session he could tell me there was only light. The fourth session was to be his last and Spirit comforted him by saying that everything would be all right. My room was literally filled with Spirit for this final session. There were many angels and loved ones. He even himself saw the angels and described one magnificent being. He had seen a rainbow behind it and I could share that this is a wonderful sign of blessings and love.

I never charge for these types of healing. The woman and then the young man hugged me as I confidently told them both that everything was going to work out. I used to think often about this young man and there one day at the dairy he tapped me on the shoulder and asked if I remembered him. He was fine and he was back in to all things he enjoyed in this life.

Recently I was asked by a family who I knew to speak at the funeral of their beloved father and husband. I had been on live television and on the television series *Sensing Murder*, but this was the hardest thing I have ever had to do. The church was packed with people and to hear the Priest say,

"Sue Nicholson will now speak about this person."

I had met him a few times and he was a lovely man. I stood up in that pew and said,

"A lot of people here today will not understand what I have to say. I am a Spiritual Medium, and for those who do not know what that means, it is that I am able talk to those who have passed over to the other side. I would just like to say that he is not in that coffin and that he is standing right there next to it. This is what he wants to say."

You could see people looking at each other and nudging each other. I was so afraid. Spirit said to me,

"Look beyond the faces. You are not doing this for the people that don't understand it. You are doing it for the family."

Well I wasn't ready for what he had to say.

"A lot of people that are here today thought I was a right so and so. But that's okay." On he went.

I finished up with,

"I just want you to know that he lives on in your memories and your heart. He is still here but in another dimension."

At the end I had to go down the aisle with all these people looking at me. I went in for a cup of tea and you could have cut the air with a knife. I could not stay and just had to get out of there. I look forward to the day when this form of tribute will be the accepted norm.

I see my work as a psychic medium as bringing reassurance to people that loved ones who have passed over are there, they are around them and they are happy. Spirit wants us to be happy. I remember saying to a person who was crying who had passed over as they were coming through from the other side,

"Why are you crying? Are you sad because you want to come back?" And they said,

"No, I am crying because I am at peace and it is the most

wonderful place. I am crying for my family who are still there and upset but I want them to know my pain and illness have gone now and I am in a better place."

Everyday is a new learning experience for me. I learn from the people that come to see me and struggles they have in their lives and the answers that Spirit gives them. I learn from the parents who have lost their children, and children who have lost their parents. Constantly I am dealing with sadness but this helps me appreciate and understand life more. People, who come to see me, come because there are issues in their lives and they need some clarity around them.

At the end of each day I sit very quietly and I just release all I have experienced that day and then I can go home with peace in my heart. I say hello in the morning and at the end of the day I say thank you for all the words, knowledge and wisdom that has come through for each soul. I then bless my room and say good bye.

Steve's Father

The hardest part of being a Psychic Medium with a medical intuitive perspective is when it comes to one's own family and I am given information about their health. Spirit will never tell me when a person is going to pass and this is how they helped me understand this as I am often inundated with this question from people.

"Just imagine you are born with a birth certificate and your mother is handed another certificate in an envelope. This other envelope is a death certificate and she has the option of opening it or not. How would you feel about receiving that second envelope?"

"I don't think I would like it as I have children of my own," I said, "and the curiosity would always be with me as to whether to open this envelope or burn it? It would always be at the back of my mind as to how much time do my children have and I would live accordingly."

Spirit reminded me,

"It's not how long you have here it is the quality of your life that you do have and how you use it. If you were told that your life is going to end in six months some people would just sit there and procrastinate on life and go before their time. Others would use their time wisely. So this is the reason why we don't give the death certificate out."

Frank, Steve's father from England, came to live with us after his second wife passed away. He was domineering but he did have a good heart.

"Steve I have something to tell you," he was getting used to these statements from me now but this was a big one.

"Your father has leukaemia and it is very, very serious. Spirit has just told me but we are not to tell him."

Steve found this hard to believe as Frank was still very active and looked very well. Just as I was finishing a reading one day I felt this huge pressure that I must go and find Frank. I said to the woman,

"I have to go now my father-in-law who lives with us is very sick. Spirit is telling me I need to go to him."

When I got into the main part of the house, Frank had collapsed on the floor. I called an ambulance and he went off to hospital. We were in the emergency room when the doctor came in. Frank was drifting in and out of consciousness. I turned to the woman doctor and said to her,

"You need to check right away. He's got leukaemia."

"Who are you?" she said, "Are you a doctor?"

I couldn't tell her that Spirit was telling me what the problem with Frank was.

The doctor was bending over talking to him saying,

"We are going to take some blood samples Mr Nicholson. Do you know your blood type?"

I piped up, "It's B positive." I had no idea but Spirit was telling me this.

At this moment Steve walked in and the doctor asked me,

"Are you sure that it is B positive?"

The doctor left the room and Steve turned to me and said,

"Are you sure Frank is B positive?"

I said, "I don't know they just told me."

The doctor came back in and began doing many tests. Again I couldn't help myself.

"He has leukaemia. Have you checked for leukaemia?" Her look told me that I was to mind my own business and let them do the work. She came back after a while and bent over Frank and said,

"Mr Nicholson we are going to admit you now and you need five units of blood."

I looked at her, "He has got leukaemia hasn't he?"

"I was just going to tell you that and also he doesn't have very long."

Frank was moved into a hospice. We got the call late one night that he was going downhill fast. When we arrived he was in a coma. Even though a person looks as though they cannot hear, they actually can and so we have to watch what we are saying.

"Words are of sound and also vibration from the mind. Thoughts that go out are energy."

I sat there holding his hand and talking to him. He was extremely hot and I got a flannel to cool him down.

"He wants the blankets off," I said, "He is telling me telepathically."

There was a woman in extreme pain next door who

was screaming.

"What a shame that woman is in so much pain," Frank began telling me.

And I replied in my mind,

'Yes thank goodness you are not in any pain.'

I held his hand and closed my eyes.

All of a sudden I was being taken with him as he went out of his body on one of his journeys to review his life. It was just like watching a movie.

It was a sunny day and he was in a large field with what appeared to be like hay all around. He was eight years old again and had long woolly trousers with braces and an old shirt on. He had a paper kite and he was running along with it and laughing. He was so joyous. All of a sudden he shot back into his body. I jumped and Steve said to me,

"Has he gone?"

"That was amazing. I went with him as he was reminiscing. No, he is not ready to go just yet."

Frank then became very cold and I put the blankets on him again.

We went out for a cup of tea and hadn't been long gone when I knew we had to go back to Frank. His breathing was getting slower and I said to the nurse,

"It won't be long now."

Then his sister and mother in Spirit appeared in the room.

I said to Steve,

"It won't be long now. They are here. They are coming to get him. Your grandmother is here."

"Steve, go and get the nurse."

Steve went to the next room to find the nurse and came back hurriedly saying,

"She is very busy with another patient."

"You do need to get her and tell her it is any second now."

As Steve walked out the door there was this tunnelling wind sound as all his energy was going up. I could see it. All these lights were gathering and pushing the energy out and up. When the nurse and Steve did arrive I could tell them that he had passed. The nurse checked and confirmed this.

"He is still here. He is still in the room." The nurse looked at me in a strange way as I said this.

He was hovering as the energy was collecting.

"Well, where is he?" Steve asked looking all around the room trying to see him.

"He is still here, the energy is still collecting."

Then he was gone.

I felt a great privilege being with Frank as he passed and actually watching what a person goes through. This was the first time I had ever had this experience. I could tell Steve that he was now happy and that he was at peace.

At the funeral of Frank we, as a family, were all gathered around the coffin, crying. Janneke my grand daughter who was five at the time looked at each one of us trying to work out our grief. She was very close to Frank, her great-grandfather and used to love to come and visit him. After the cremation, Janneke asked if she could travel in my car back home. It was just me and her and as we were driving along she turned to me and said,

"Nana, why was everybody crying?"

"Because your great-granddad has gone."

"No he hasn't." She said, eyes wide open,

"He was standing right by the box. He is not gone Nana."

She looked at me and profoundly said,

"They live around us and it is called heaven. People shouldn't cry because they haven't gone, they are still with us."

Here was this very old soul talking to me.

"He told me Nana that he has to go and have a rest and he will come back when he is ready and when he is stronger."

The following year he returned to us on Steve's birthday. When living with us Frank would sit on the back deck having a smoke and he was unable to give up even though we used to tell him how it was no good for his health.

"I am going to go any way, so what does it matter?" he would often say to us.

I was in the kitchen looking outside at Steve enjoying his day with our daughters and our grandchildren when I saw Frank's misty form appear. I called out to Steve,

"Your father is sitting out there on the deck with you all."

Frank was sitting there in Spirit, laughing and having a smoke.

"I have a present for Steve," he told me and proceeded

to say what it was.

Every year when he lived with us he would give Steve some money and tell him 'to have a drink on me and buy something nice for yourself.'

I said to Steve,

"Your dad has bought you a present. He tells me he has bought a Lotto ticket. It's behind the television. It is going to win."

We went and had a look and there behind the television was this old Lotto ticket. I took it to the shop and it had won nearly one hundred dollars. That was Frank's present to Steve.

Sensitivity to Spirit Increases

The call came through on my answering machine one day from a company called Ninox Productions. They said they had heard about me and that they were looking for psychics who were prepared to work on a television series. They gave out no more information. Television was certainly quite different from anything I was doing and I felt very hesitant about phoning them back and so I asked Spirit,

"What is this all about? Can I do this?"

"Give them a call," Spirit said, *"You will be able to do this and you have nothing to lose."*

When I rang Ninox they explained to me that they had been looking for psychics throughout New Zealand to work on a programme. The series would involve psychics looking into past unsolved murders in New Zealand. They had asked at Spiritualist Churches and found out who was working professionally in this way. My name kept on coming up. If I was interested I was to come in and do a test. Of course I was very, very nervous as I was putting myself and my abilities on the line and as usual my deepest, darkest self belief issues rose quickly to the surface.

The first test was to give the production journalist a reading. Everything was correct. I could have told her more but thought that would be too much information and she would not appreciate it. I had passed the first test. Next I was given a photo of a person and I was asked to work with it. The girl in the photo appeared and she was just standing there.

"It is about me."

I said to the journalists in the room,

"Quick I need a pen and paper, she's here and I want to start writing with her."

The information came through extremely quickly as she had been waiting to tell her story and for someone on this side to help her. Olive Walker was the name she gave me. When I had finished channelling the owner of Ninox came in and all I heard was,

"Okay, we will let you know."

I got back in the car absolutely exhausted. I said to myself,

"I don't know if I can do this even if they wanted me and I did get the job."

All the way as I drove to watch my daughter play golf in Palmerston North, I kept thinking about it. And I heard Spirit say,

"You are going to do this! We all have seasons in our lives and sometimes the time is right for us to grow and blossom. Each one of us is the seedling that is just lying dormant waiting to break through the ground and be noticed. Let the light of Spirit nurture you and guide you to branch out in directions you never thought possible. Grow from your deepest roots and that part of your soul where you reach above any

weeds that surround you, will conquer all darkness and attain the heights of what you came here to do."

When I returned to Wellington, Ninox phoned me up to tell me that they were really interested in me and would like to employ me. First of all I would be a consultant and my job would be to interview many psychics from around the country and then select one to work with me on this new series to be called *Sensing Murder*.

The tables had now turned and each interviewee had to give me a reading. This certainly sorted out who was strong in this field and who wasn't. Some had been videoed as I was unable to get to every city and this is how I found the person. Besides what I was seeing and hearing I also checked out each psychic's aura and through the colours I was able to confirm my selection as to their authenticity. Being a consultant certainly gave me the confidence that I was able to do the programme.

The first experience of being 'A Sensing Murder Psychic' was challenging. A week before I was told which day I would be required for work. It was hectic as then I had to rearrange appointments I had made with clients. The night before I would receive the time to be at the airport but information of the destination I would not know until I turned up at the counter and asked for my ticket. For the second series when I turned up at the counter one day, the counter person said,

"Aren't you Sue Nicholson from Sensing Murder? Why don't you know where you are going? Hasn't the other side told you?"

I could tell her,

"There is a whole lot of trust involved as not only do my bosses on this side give me no information but my bosses on the other side will not tell me either! If I did know the programme would not be authentic and people could say we research the information before we go. The challenge for me is to get it correct through Spirit. I am also not allowed to work on any cases in my area."

When I finally do arrive at the destination I am taken to a hotel room set-up for recording. After pleasantries, we get straight into it. Sometimes they give me a photo and sometimes they don't and the session will go all day. Going on location to trace the last steps of the person's life happens after the initial gathering of information from Spirit. Usually I am flown home again that day and it takes me a number of days to come right as I am mentally and physically exhausted when I arrive home.

As I sat on the plane one day after having worked on the Tracey-Ann Patient case in Auckland I closed my eyes to rest hoping no-one would talk to me. I was in an aisle seat and I felt someone standing next to me wanting my attention. I opened my eyes and there was Tracey-Ann. She thanked me for allowing her to come through and tell her story. She had been waiting a very long time. She then walked down the plane, turned around, waved and was gone.

When a child is brutally murdered or abducted, some people say they must have done something bad in a previous life. I have tremendous difficulty getting my head around this as I don't believe it is Karmic where we are in a payback situation. 'How could anyone do this to a child?' I always ask. Maybe I won't understand this until I pass over and get the perspective from the other side.

People often ask why don't our angels protect us and how could anybody kill anybody else? Spirit explained,

"Every soul in the Universe has a destiny. Whether a child comes to earth and takes one breath and passes over or whether they live to a hundred years they touch many lives and there are lessons to be learnt. When someone passes brutally it may get the family or even the community closer together. Out of the situation something will come out more positively and it will make people look at life in a different way."

I have dealt with a number of cases where the child has been run over and when the child comes through they don't hold any anger against the person as it is not for them to carry. Holding onto how they passed is not going to help with their own healing. This is a life lesson for us here on Earth as when people hurt us here on earth we can either be pulled down by it or we can grow and move on from it.

All the cases I have worked on in Sensing Murder have been extremely hard but the case of Agnes in particular affected me as I was drawn to how she had been so cruelly treated. She was a twelve year old girl who had been brutally assaulted and then drowned as she was being chased. Her information was extremely clear and came in very strong.

On the way home in the plane I still felt her strongly with me. Her energy had attached on to mine as on the other side, she was still afraid and very lonely. When you work on a case I have found they don't want to leave you as it is though they are reliving their life again through someone else and at long last they have a voice.

The programme was filmed on the Sunday and I was back at work with clients on the Monday. As usual I was not feeling too well and thought in a few days I would be right. However this time by Thursday when I went to do my regular morning show on TV, people noticed that I didn't look well and by Friday I felt very ill and I gave in and went home from work. I couldn't get my breath and couldn't go to bed for the night as lying down was impossible.

On the Saturday I had an appointment with a private investigator who was interested in working with me and I struggled through the two hours feeling absolutely dreadful. Afterwards I had to go somewhere else and as I was driving on the motorway my head kept hitting the steering wheel. I was so exhausted. Spirit said to me,

"You have to go to the doctors now ."

"No I haven't got the time. I will come right, I always do. I just want to go home and sleep."

"You can't go home you must go to the doctors."

I decided to call into the doctors on the way home and as happens in my life she had a free appointment to see me.

I was admitted to the hospital straight away from the doctors. My oxygen levels were so low that if I had gone home where there was no one there and gone to bed I would have gone into a coma and died. They had trouble getting my oxygen levels up even after they had given me a lot of medication.

I never know in any situation I am in, when Spirit will see the need for me to assist somebody. I have discovered this to be the case whether I am sick or not. I had only been in hospital for a day when late at night a new woman patient was admitted. After they had settled her down, I could still hear that she wasn't breathing normally. I struggled up out of bed and said to her,

"Are you okay, do you want anything?"

"I can't get my breath. I have been in and out of this hospital, for six months now and I can't get whatever it is off my chest."

"I am a psychic medium, would you like some help as to what is happening to you?" I felt she would be open to this.

Spirit told me,

"She has had a set of twins earlier on in her life and they have died. It is time for this woman to let go."

"You have been grieving constantly for your babies and held all your sad thoughts in for so long. Know your twin babies are in a happy place," I said.

All of a sudden she started to gag and began to try and bring something up. I got a bowl off the shelf and then up came a large amount of gunk from her chest. The nurse came in and was not happy that I was out of bed helping another patient. The nurse pulled the curtains and I could hear them talking about what had happened. The patient told the nurse,

"I couldn't get my breath and this lady came over and

helped me. She told me many things about my life. Look at what I have brought up from my lungs. This is the first time in six months I have been able to breathe freely like this."

There is always an emotional background to all illnesses, whether from a past life or this life.

On the fourth day, I couldn't get up out of bed, I was so weak.

"Why am I not getting any better? What's happening here?" I asked Spirit.

I kept seeing Agnes in my mind's eye. That night as I tried to sleep sitting up in bed, I opened my eyes and I was looking through a set of eyes that were not mine. I said to Spirit,

"Whose are these eyes?"

"It is her eyes, Agnes has not left you," they said.

"You can not stay here little one, you can not stay. You are making me ill," I told her.

That night I went to sleep and I was taken over to the other side. I believe that I felt so ghastly and depleted that I was ready to pass over. I had lost the will to stay.

A friend who had recently passed was waiting for me. She kept her distance from me and kept saying,

"You can't stay. You can't stay."

She kept on walking further away from me.

"I only want a hug," was all I could say.

"You can't stay here Sue, you have to go back. There are many things yet that you have to finish and I am still healing."

"You look so good."

"I am good. Tell everyone that I am well and that I am healing and when I am ready, I will come back and they will know that I am there."

The other side was so peaceful. All of a sudden I was back in the room and in bed gasping for air. The nurse came and checked my oxygen levels. They had dropped dramatically.

The next night Agnes was still with me. I asked her to go towards the light and told her she couldn't stay with me. I asked all those in Spirit to help me. As I was asking that, the whole area of my bed became this most beautiful purple colour. This is the highest of colours and I know it is Spirit's colour. It was like this blanket of love had been placed over me. Right down at the bottom of my bed I saw Jesus. He was standing there and he said to me,

"Close your eyes. All will be well."

That was the first full night's sleep I had in ages. The next morning when I woke up, I could breathe. I took the oxygen tube out of my nose as I didn't need it anymore. When the doctors came around, they checked my levels and they were right up. He felt I could leave as long as I could take care of myself. I said goodbye to my little girl and my friend as it was time for us all to move on, so each of us could heal in our own ways.

People ask why, if I do healing then why can't I heal myself? Sometimes things are way beyond my capabilities and there is always the value of the experiences we go through in life to assist us with our own personal growth. I feel that something dramatic had to happen such as this illness to learn to protect myself more and also, so I could heal with regards to my friend's sudden passing by going over to the other side to see her. This is the way Spirit works.

Taking One's Life

Spirit has taught me to know that no matter how dark you feel within your life, there is always a glimmer of hope. The light that Spirit will bring through will transform into a brightness that you can trust and bring through into your life.

"You fill a room with darkness from your own fears. By lighting a match that one small flame will illuminate the whole room and that will pierce the darkness."

In earlier times I had not been able to light that match and had wanted to go from this earthly existence. I did try to leave early but thankfully Spirit would not allow me to pass over. This however is not the case for everyone. We all do have free will and usually Spirit cannot override that.

Here in New Zealand more and more people especially young ones are finishing this lifetime before it is supposed to be ended. They see it as the only way out. My role, Spirit has told me, is to assist and counsel these despairing souls in staying, understanding how the other side works and then encouraging them to complete their life mission. The many people who come through from the other side who have passed by taking their own lives generally all wish to come back and complete their lives. They often say to me,

"I have found the answer over here so quickly and easily. If only I had been able to look at the problem in a different way."

Some souls will reincarnate back very quickly after suicide, often into that family setting. Others will wait until their loved ones pass over and they have been able to connect again. The time it takes to heal and come to terms with what they have done depends on each individual soul and how willing they are to heal.

Spirit gives a message to all those reading this book:

"Taking one's life is not the solution to one's problems and what is going on around you. Find the solution to your life's problem and know that you have a lot to live for. Ask for help from those that can assist you. There is a way out."

Sometimes we get down in that space, and we cannot see very far. Our angels and guides are always with us to help. So people will ask,

"Why are the angels letting people take their lives then?"

When we come here they are commissioned to us and they are with us till we pass over, but they also know that we have freewill. They don't want us to take our lives but they know that if we are in so much pain and the will is so strong there is nothing they can do.

My friend, who I saw on the other side when I was in hospital, had been my friend before she passed over. Our friendship grew out of the first meeting when she came for a reading. One day she asked if I could help her and I could tell she was very depressed and down and she needed information from Spirit. She had been unwell with terrible headaches and was feeling that no-one believed her. She asked me,

"Please tell me Sue is this real or is it all in my head?"

"You are not well and it is not your imagination. The antidepressants that they have put you on as they say it is your imagination, are changing your personality."

"I can't carry on anymore," she said, "I don't want to live with this pain anymore."

"You can do this. We will sort something out. I will phone your doctor up and get some help."

"They don't listen to me," was all she could say over and over again.

"She needs a brain scan. There will be an appointment available at her doctors," my Chinese doctor guide cut in.

I phoned up and there had been a cancellation. I told my friend that when she went to the doctors she was not to leave until she had an appointment for the scan. On that night she let me know she had an appointment for the scan in two weeks time, but this was too far away she said.

"Sue, I don't know if I can wait that long as the pain is too much. I don't know if I can go on."

Exactly a week after I saw her, she hung herself. I was absolutely devastated and felt so helpless that I hadn't done enough for her. I had to go to do my segment on television that day and I really didn't think I was up to it. Next I heard her voice saying,

"You must go on."

I did the show and afterwards I sat in my car in the car park and spoke to her and asked her why?

"I am happy now, I am happy." Waiting for another week was impossible. *Can you speak to my husband and daughter and tell them what I have said. Can you go to the funeral home to see if I look okay?"*

It was strange because I speak to people who pass over all the time, but I have never seen a friend in a coffin. All day I was nervous thinking about seeing her. The funeral home was to shut at five and I would be finishing work at four thirty. I kept messing about and trying to put it off. Thinking 'if I leave it long enough they will be shut' but deep inside I knew I had to do this. I went to the funeral home and he said they would wait for me outside the door as it was nearly closing time. I walked up to the coffin and looked in to see her. She looked at peace. I began talking to her as I was bent over the coffin telling her how good she looked.

"Why are you looking down there, when I am standing right beside you?"

"Wow they have done your hair good," I said and we both began to laugh and laugh. The only problem being, the funeral director couldn't hear her, only me! Goodness knows what the people thought when I came out of that room.

That night, as I went home she asked me to talk for her, to her husband and daughter. I arranged to meet them the next day. Sometimes passed loved ones will ask me to go out and buy something for their family member. I will be guided to the shop where they want me to get it from. My friend kept showing me these two engraved rose quartz crystal hearts. They were entwined together. I said,

"You will have to show me as I had never seen them before."

She told me where to go and the name of the shop. I went in and looked around and couldn't see them.

"Are you sure they are in this shop?"

"Can I help you?" the sales assistant said to me.

"I am looking for these engraved heart rose quartz crystals that are entwined together."

"I have just put something like that in the window yesterday," the assistant said.

She got them out and asked me if they were the ones. I said,

"I'll just check."

"Is that the ones?" I stupidly said out loud to my friend.

My friend confirmed they were and the shop assistant looked at me as though I was just off another planet. She was more bemused when I told her I was talking to someone from the other side that had just passed away, and this was a gift for her husband on this side.

I was taken to another shop to purchase a beautifully engraved mirror with words about mothers on it for the daughter. When I gave them the gifts I also gave them the gift of my friend's channelled words for them. They were grieving and very angry but this meeting did provide a little comfort.

Some people are constantly attempting to end their lives but for whatever reason it does not happen. This man who came to see me was one such case.

"You know you are not supposed to go over there," I

said to him.

His mother came through and confirmed what I said,

"You are not coming over here. It was me who sent that boar!"

Unbeknown to me he had gone into the bush to finish his life.

He was sitting there in contemplation when all of a sudden this massive boar with huge tusks came through the opening and just looked at him. It frightened him immensely and he ran and ran until he was out. It had petrified him.

"What's that telling you? It is telling you that they don't want you to go, there is more for you to do," I said.

When I am walking in many different shoes I never know why I am put in places but I always have to trust it is for a reason. The nurses when I was in hospital with pneumonia, I know were intrigued by me but didn't want to bother me. I used to lie there and look at their auras. One nurse seemed to have a lot of sadness around her and so I said to Spirit,

"Find a way that I can talk to her without me forcing myself on her."

She would come around but look at me very strangely as though she was frightened of me. The next day she was working with another nurse and they were taking all the sheets off the bed next to me. I could see her glancing at me all the time. The other nurse started asking me about *Sensing Murder* and we struck up a conversation. I could feel that the sad nurse did not believe in what I did and finally she said so. Later on the other nurse went off duty and as the sad nurse was serving my evening meal, I said,

"You have a great sadness and I don't know what Spirit means but they want me to tell you that your son won't do it again."

She burst out crying. I continued,

"There is a lady here in Spirit, she is not your mother, but she is your birth mother as you are adopted."

The truth was all there for her and she relented and began to listen.

"Can I bring a photo in of my son? I don't want to disturb you as I know you are sick."

I agreed and thought the quietness of the night, when I am unable to sleep, would be the perfect time to be in touch with what is going on for her son. With the photo the next night I channelled pages of information to help her, her son and her family. When she came on duty the next day I asked her to read it. I thought it important also that her son read it. She was on the afternoon shift the next day and when she came in she said,

"I couldn't believe what you wrote. My son has read it, but my husband is not sure about it but I have left it there for him to read. It's up to him."

At six o'clock that night he came in to see me. He shook my hand and said thank you that their son had read it, understood the messages and he wouldn't try to take his life again.

Every night as the nurse was going home she had this overwhelming feeling that her son was hanging from the garage and she was trying to get him down. As she left everyday for work she was worried that he would not be alive when she arrived home. From that night she started to come into work smiling and happy.

Another nurse who worked the next shift from midnight till dawn asked me one night, "What do you do?" She did not have a clue and Spirit told me she was very religious. I said,

"You will not understand this, but I am a Spiritual Medium."

You could see her energy shift backwards and she said to me,

"I don't believe in people like you. In my religion it is evil."

"That's okay and that's your opinion," I said, "but there are a lot of things that Spirit wants to say to you and your grandmother is right here right now."

"What is she saying?"

"You have to go out there soon as a patient will call you, but give me your watch I will hold it and through psychometry your grandmother will tell me. We can do it with photographs, or jewellery or any object. I have even read a hub cap, the only thing left from a burnt out car."

As soon as she passed me the watch she was called to an emergency. She looked at me as to how did I know what was going to happen next. Anyway I wrote pages and pages for her. I gave them to her the next evening she came in. She was talking to the other nurse who had the reading and she asked her,

"Have you said anything to the psychic lady about

me?"

The other nurse replied that she hadn't. She said, "I can't believe what she knows about me and what she has written."

Well after that they all started to come round like moths to a light. They would ask me if I needed anything, they would pat my bed down.

I was meant to be in there to give readings to those that needed them and to help the woman who had the breathing difficulties, as well as the nurses. You are put in places not knowing why at the time, but by staying with it you will always see the reasons for it and the learning gained.

One night quite late I had Archangel Gabriel come through.

"Write this poem down as in time it will be read all over the world."

At the time I couldn't understand what Gabriel was telling me. How could I write a poem and have it published when I had so much difficulty with learning when I was at school? Having this poem read by people all over the world was way beyond what I might possibly ever imagine. Before I could question my abilities any longer I found a piece of paper and a pen and the words began to flow through me. After completing the message the angel asked me to keep it in a safe place. I went to bed.

"Pick up that magazine," I heard Spirit say to me as I was standing at the checkout at my local supermarket a few weeks later.

It was an overseas magazine that I never ever buy and when I asked Spirit about this they said,

"There is something important for you in this magazine."

Not knowing what I was supposed to be looking for I flicked through the pages until I heard them say stop. There was a notice asking if anyone had a poem that if accepted would be published in *The International Library of Poetry–Honoured Poets of 1998*.

My poem was selected and now it is and has been read by many people. I keep this book with me when doing readings as often Spirit will ask me to read to family members this poem when somebody close to them has taken their lives. The grieving partners and family members find much comfort in the words and it is like their soul understands the course they are to take from this point on.

In The Darkest Hour

When the skies are blue, but there's darkness all about
Just think of me as your light,
Just ask for help and I will be there,
Because I am the guardian of your light.
Through your eyes you will see me
As I am your angel in the darkest night.
As I watch over you when you sleep,
I will protect you as you sleep.
I will let no harm come unto you.
When times are hard and tears will flow,
I will wrap my wings around you and let my love flow.
So don't give up, my beautiful one,
As we are not to meet just yet.
There will be a time when we will unite,
But until then, I will see that only
Joy and love will surround you.

Requests for Help

Ever since the first series of *Sensing Murder* was shown I have been inundated with requests to assist people with situations where they feel something untoward has happened to a loved one or person they know. I have tramped through the hills up behind Lower Hutt looking for a missing person, I have been taken to various sites around Wellington, had requests from the French Police and even been asked to go to Fiji before I was able to solve it from here in New Zealand.

A woman came to me looking for help as her cousin had been murdered. There were no clues as to who had done this and no one had been arrested. I do have a long waiting list but in desperate cases such as this I will always assist. She arrived with another woman to take notes as she was extremely nervous and frightened and had no experience of psychic mediums before. She had brought in a photo of her cousin and I placed it upside down on the table.

After I explained what I do and commenced my customary prayer the room was filled with Spirit. Her grandfather came through. Often when I am working with a new client and they have no experience of how I work, Spirit will come through and give some information that only they would know. This time it was about a miscarriage the murdered man's wife had ten years previous. I could see the goose bumps appear on the two women in front of me.

Then the young man that was murdered came through.

"I was being watched and followed all the time and I had received some threatening phone calls but had told no one. I didn't want my new wife who had just had a baby to worry. I came home that night and was attacked and killed right outside my front door on the pathway."

Fiji kept on coming up for me. "Yes it has happened in Fiji," I said.

The young passed over man was intensifying his urgency with what he was telling me. He had the line to communicate and it was all coming out.

I began drawing the street where he lived and noting important sites where it had all happened. First it was the uncle's house.

"Uncle, uncle!" he kept on saying to me, *"He lives close to me, he has yellow roses in the garden and the men have also been threatening him by phone."* I began drawing the school in the street and then he said,

"One of the men that killed me went to the school."

Then I was being shown exactly how it had all happened. I was literally transported to the scene to watch it unfold.

"I can see the cars arrive, their headlights are on. Five men get out. There are two cars, light blue and green. One of the drivers is getting out of the car and running towards the gate. He is grabbing your cousin and now he is being stabbed. He is stabbed through the lung and he is screaming." I felt the knife go through my own lung. "The family are coming out to see what is going on. He is dying and he has his head on someone's lap. I am now seeing the funeral and one of the killers is here and even sympathising with the family."

I continued to draw and tell where the others lived.

"No more will happen. Tell your uncle that he can stop fearing for the safety of his family. The men responsible for this will be found."

The two women who came confirmed what I said about the family and the way her cousin had passed. This information assisted the uncle in Fiji and eventually the Fijian Police were able to arrest those involved.

I still have to pinch myself to think that I have been chosen to be involved in a programme such as *Sensing Murder*. I often look at it and think why me? I know in time I will have completed my time with working with such a programme and Spirit will move me on to something else. I feel besides the wonderful assistance and peace that we have given to the families of the victims we have also ensured a huge audience of many people have come to believe and understand that there is actually more to our physical life than what we know at present. For the first *Sensing Murder Series* to have had the largest audience ever for a new series opener and to have won the *Qantas Television Media Award* is a testament to this.

I feel so proud, privileged and blessed to have been

chosen to bring through messages from those that have passed and to be involved in such a programme. It has been a hard journey and a lot of pressure with a lot of sadness but if just one murder is solved then it has all been worth it. My confidence and abilities have grown with each episode I have been involved with and the channel lines of communication have become extremely clear.

Ninox recently began to make a documentary about my life and how I work. As House Blessings are a major part of what I do, they wanted this to be included. A hairdresser had approached Ninox to ask if I could be contacted to cleanse the premises of her business. The salon had been converted from an old house which originally had been the house of an elderly man, George, who had been murdered. Ninox decided this would provide the perfect situation for the segment.

This case had been covered on the first series of *Sensing Murder* but I had not been involved as it was in my home town. I did not remember the murder nor did I know anything about it as I was actually living in England at the time. The night it had shown on TV last year I had gone out and even though I had tried to video the programme, the video did not work. Spirit is very capable of ensuring that our life unfolds as it should and there is no such thing as coincidence. So I had no knowledge of what had gone on in this house.

Whatever building I go into I pick up many peoples energy; those of the living as well as the past. As soon as I arrived at the salon the old man called George in Spirit greeted me. Walking through the house I was able to tell the television crew and interviewer what had gone on as George was particularly clear and gave me a lot of information. One room was exceptionally horrible. It was where he had been bashed and I could see what had happened to him.

I began the blessing using Tibetan bells as I moved from room to room. When the Tibetan bells are hit together the beautiful high sound vibration will shatter any negative energy and will return it to a higher vibration. Our world is made up of energy vibrating within and all around us and sometimes these vibrations can become blocked when there is a stale stagnant energy in a place. I combine this sound with incense, sage and the sacred symbols of Reiki so the energies in the house or office will be lightened and cleared. Reiki symbols are positive energy and I put these in and outside the house so any negative energy cannot get in.

"Someone working in this salon has had a severe ear problem," I said as it was hurting my ear. One of the girls confirmed that she had recently had an ear infection. I went into the next room and I could hear this very loud and unusual music. The house owners laughed as this room was where a young woman from Africa did braiding. She always played her music so loud and it was deafening to everyone. I walked past a chair in the tea room and said,

"Someone always sits in that chair and has tremendous headaches.

"Oh that is so and so and yes she always has headaches," the hairdresser said.

"It is coming from her neck and she is going to have that

fixed soon and it will be fine," Spirit told me.

Well the young woman came in and confirmed she was off to the chiropractor. The people in the salon were now firmly convinced I was for real and followed me with intrigue.

Next I walked into the laundry. The lights began to flicker and everyone started to say it was him.

"It's George," they all said.

It was not, much to their disappointment. I could tell them that it's the electrics and recently a man went up into the ceiling. It had been a Telephone man fixing the lines and he had interfered with other wires.

"You know what I've got to tell everybody. I never had any money you know." George was with me and I began saying aloud what he was telling me.

"I don't know why they've got my floor up in the room where I was killed because it wasn't in the floor boards."

The camera crew were staring in amazement at me as the floor boards had been lifted previously but this segment had never been included in the screening of *Sensing Murder*.

"They thought I had money in the ceiling, well I got nothing up there, but I will tell you where the little treasure that I did have is."

He was laughing his head off and then he showed me this really old tin that looked like a biscuit tin and he said it was a chocolate tin.

"It is outside under the concrete tile now. Come outside and I will show you."

As he pointed and said it is there, I couldn't see anything. There was grass and the others started ripping it off. Underneath the grass was this concrete tile.

"This was my lovely garden," he said, *"You know what, they killed me because they thought I had lots of money and I didn't. In the tin were a few old medals."*

Since I blessed these premises and met George, more information has come to light which is being worked on with the Police.

Often people will contact me and tell me of the noises they hear or of some presence that they can feel in their home or office.

"Am I imagining this? Is there something I can do about it? Can you help me?" Are the first questions asked when people have finally found someone who does believe and does not think they are going crazy. To be able to tell someone who will actually accept as true their concerns and is prepared to do something about it, is a huge and relieving step to take for many people.

Throughout history these presences have been portrayed as ghosts but to me they are Spirit who are not yet at rest. Something traumatic may have happened to them and they were just not ready to go across to the other side and so they remain in limbo.

Most people feel afraid and frightened of these presences, even though they do not always physically see them, as they feel they are not in control of their home or office. Having an intruder in your home or office is how people describe it and calling the Police is not an option! That is why I have the nickname of 'policewoman for the other side.' Often if nothing is done about clearing these presences over to the other side things will get worse.

During a reading for a woman I was able to tell her that her little girl is always saying there is a man in her room in the house. The man is the previous owner of the house who has passed over, I told her and he is trying to get you out of that house as he still believes it is his. He does not want you there.

"Have you noticed how the arguments between you and your partner have increased and appear to be getting worse?" I asked. "Presences can influence our moods and how we are feeling."

"My partner has seen this man in the house," she confirmed.

It was a hot lovely day in November when I went around to bless their home. When I went inside the house was like a fridge. It was freezing. "It is cold all the time," the woman said.

I walked into the kitchen.

"He is here and he is very annoyed. He and his wife built this house and with their two children they lived here for many years."

He started to tell me,

"You have moved the kitchen around," and he described how it used to be.

The woman began apologising,

"Oh we didn't mean to offend him. Shall we move it back then?"

"You are the owner of the house now and you are the boss. This is your house, not his." This woman needed to be strong so the presence would leave.

As I was saying this 'the man' became angry and went

up the hallway to the daughter's bedroom.

"Why are you in here?" I asked him.

"This is my room. It's where I used to sleep. I didn't sleep in the same room as my wife."

"You need to go to the light. You are not going to stay here," I strongly told him.

I cleansed the hallway and then went into the daughter's room. It was the weirdest thing and it is the only time I have had this happen in a house blessing.

I was in front of the doorway to the daughter's bedroom and as I went to walk in he stood right in front of me. I could literally feel his hands on me. I said to the woman who was following me,

"He won't let me in."

The woman looked strangely at me because she couldn't see or sense him.

"I am not frightened of you. I have met bigger things than you. You don't scare me." I commandingly said out loud as I knew fear would breed more fear.

All of a sudden he pushed me against the wall. If that person was not there watching me, nobody would have believed me.

"Is that all that you can do, that doesn't frighten me."

The woman was petrified. I managed to get into the room. I had the incense burning and I was just over by the bed doing the Reiki symbols when he took the incense out of my hand and it was floating across the room. We both looked at it and couldn't believe it. It dropped on the bed quilt. That was it.

"Right you are going!"

All of a sudden this lady appeared.

"Who are you?" I asked.

"I am really sorry but that is my husband," she said in such a gentle, soft way.

He started to argue with her and I could see that he had been this way with her all their earthly time together.

"He has to go towards the light. He has to go to the other side. Please show him the way."

I finished off cleansing the house and he appeared in the kitchen and apologised.

"Why have you stayed on?" I asked him.

"When I died I left the house to my two children and they sold it. I wanted the house kept and when the new people took over the house, they began to change it. This made me angry and so I began taking it out on the people that live here. I couldn't accept I had gone. I thought this was still my house and I really wanted to talk to my children."

Sometimes people do not accept they have gone and want to complete what they see as 'unfinished business'. He didn't mean to be horrible to this family but he actually needed to talk to his children about what had happened to the house. After this he was gone.

The woman asked the neighbours about the previous owners and what they heard confirmed all that I told them. When he went the house became still, it warmed up and you could definitely feel the difference in the energy in the house. When we went into the lounge the young daughter was playing with her dolls. We heard her say to them,

"It is okay now because that man has gone. He's gone

and he's not here any more."

There is also the darker energy of lower level Spirit that can come through to visit people which I pickup on in House Blessings. On the other side it is not all goodness, love and light. This can be the 'scary side' of what we can experience in life sometimes. If a person is still in misery when they pass over or something that is haunting them hasn't been cleared then that person will resonate at a lower, darker energy level and they can continue to be on the earth plane looking to disrupt.

Sprits in limbo always seem to know when I am coming and their activity gets much stronger. The daughter of a friend of mine had started flatting with two other girls and she kept seeing a youngish man in her doorway. His energy started to frighten her as he would come in to her room, sit on the bed and start touching her.

When I arrived at the flat there was a dead bird at the back door. They had no cat. I went into the house and I lit the incense. She had been vacuuming the hallway just before I arrived and by the front door she had rolled up a finely woven rug outside her bedroom. We were talking away and I was giving her a message when I said to her,

"Can you smell burning?"

The rolled up rug behind us was on fire, right inside of it. There was no way it could have been started by us. We ran into the kitchen, got some water and put the fire out.

"What is this all about?" the woman asked. I said,

"He doesn't want me to be here, he is trying to

frighten me, so he is doing anything he can to make me go away."

I was drawn to go to the bathroom next. I walked into this small bathroom and looking into the mirror I saw the man and this was where he had killed himself. The information I received about him was that he was a stalker and he had been badly sexually abused as a young person. This could explain why this woman felt him touching her while she was in bed.

As I moved onto the young woman's bedroom next, he followed me. It had been his bedroom. I told him to go to the light with the help of his loved ones and others there in Spirit. He did go. House Blessings are an example of clearing this denser energy and assisting them to go to the light.

It is a fallacy to believe you need to have an old house to have energies lingering. Energies of people whether passed or living will stay behind them in houses, factories, shops, offices even in hotel rooms.

For my Fiftieth birthday, Steve and I went to Australia. It was school holidays, and there was little accommodation in the city where we had chosen to go. We finally found somewhere, it wasn't very nice, but that was all there was. I walked into the motel and out onto the deck.

"So what's wrong with this place?" Steve frustratingly asked. He knew by the way I was walking about and started to look in a particular way. He could tell by the look on my face that I wasn't happy as there was something in that motel room that I was sensing. I had not experienced such feelings of sickness in a motel ever before.

On entering the bedroom I could see the energy of somebody injecting themselves with drugs.

"There have been teenagers in here doing drugs."

"Can't you do your thing that you do? There is no where else to stay," he was so tired as we had been driving for hours and he just wanted somewhere to stop and relax.

"Haven't you got those bells with you?"

"Well I can't take everything on holiday with me!"

We went out and bought some lavender incense sticks and using the Reiki symbols we were able to cleanse the room. After returning from a meal out even Steve commented how the room felt lighter and different. The ability to sense energy always tests me when I stay in accommodation. I take or buy my own plates, cups and glasses and this habit has been known to sometimes cause a problem. I am okay with people that I know, but there are other places where I won't even have a cup of tea. I am not prepared to absorb their energy.

I was involved once with what felt like a Secret Service mission. The Human Resources person from a large corporate office asked me to secretly come in on the weekend to detail to them what was going in a part of the office where a man had committed suicide. I was to meet her at a certain place and I only had so much time before the workers would come in, in the afternoon.

Initially I went around various seats in the office and picked up on all the different people's energies. The woman was amazed and she nodded in agreement with each statement I made. I found the seat of the person who had committed suicide without being told and said what had happened. There was definitely an energy disturbance within the office. The management felt the staff were becoming paranoid. With the clearing that I did, the management contacted me later and told me that the atmosphere in the office had definitely improved and the staff were more relaxed.

We are all able to sense energy of those around us whether they are happy, sad, calm or angry. Many people speak of the feelings they get when they walk into certain rooms or offices and intuitively react to these. Our energy bodies or what is called our aura spreads out to more than five metres from our physical body and with Reiki it spreads out even further.

Children are our Future

Watching my children and their children grow and develop in understanding and accepting Spirit brings joy to my heart. The children of the future will be thankful that so many souls at this moment are opening up to Spirit and teaching the ways of the Universe. It will certainly ensure their job is a lot easier in bringing forth the wisdom of the Universe.

As my children have grown they are beginning to use their abilities to assist them with their lives and are totally awakening their children to the gifts they have. Janneke, my granddaughter, is open to all things Spiritual and at times I am amazed at what she is able to bring through. She talks to and about the angels and other areas of Spirit with deep understanding and at times endures the same tests as me. One day I got a phone call from her and she was extremely upset.

"Nana I can't help it if I am able to do things like you. I have some friends and I know they don't like me and they talk about me."

"That's okay I said you are a special girl. A lot of people don't understand what we are able to do."

"I don't have any friends or anyone to play with. I don't want to go back to school after the holidays," she began to sob.

Spirit told me to tell her,

"When you go back you will find a little girl in the playground, who is standing alone." Spirit described her,

"She has no friends as well. Go up to her and say 'would you like to be my friend?' She will be a new friend for you?"

On the Monday night she phoned me up,

"Nana, I saw the girl standing there all by herself and I went up to her and said hello my name is Janneke, what's your name? Would you like to be my friend? She said yes."

By supporting and nurturing her gifts, she will also be able to complete her contract this lifetime.

My grandson is another very old soul and before he was born my daughter asked me to ask Spirit to give her son a name. The name Khody with this unusual spelling was given to me. At the time we trusted the name Spirit had brought through for us and recently I asked Spirit why this spelling.

"The name is derived from the word coyote and it is a more modern and usable form of this word. In another life your grandson lived as a Red Indian and he had an incredibly developed sense of commitment to community and family just as a coyote does."

Being a Red Indian in a past life didn't surprise me as his favourite pastime is playing cowboys and Indians and watching these type movies in this lifetime.

When Khody was finally born, he had to be revived. After everything had calmed down and all the medical people had left I picked up Khody and put my hand on his head. Instantly, his most previous past life came through. He had been a collar wearing priest and he looked in his very early 30s. The priesthood learning is still with him and a number of times we have been surprised when this learning has come through. When he was two years old and just beginning to talk, he was in my bedroom and he looked at the picture of Jesus on the wall. I held him up to show him the picture, and I said,

"Look, man." And he said,

"No, Jesus"

Now Khody is five and not long ago at one point in the day when his great uncle was looking after him Khody's whole face changed. Khody then began talking about the book of *Revelations* and how God loves us and God is all around us. He appeared to be in a trance and quite a different person and it even amazed my brother who has studied the Bible.

Next Khody was back and asking to go out and play. When Khody was asked about what he was saying he had no recollection of what he had said. I asked my daughter if Khody had any Bible training and she said no so I asked Khody,

"Who talked to you about God?"

"No one it is just in me," he said, "I know it. I know all about him."

I watch my grandchildren and all children of the Universe and I am reminded of the beautiful words that Spirit shared with me,

"All the beautiful gardens that surround us here on the

other side can grow without the physical elements that you need on Earth. We only need to hold each flower in our hands and by giving it enduring love it will grow to be the most magnificent flower you can ever imagine.

I ask each one of you that have or are involved with children to hold, nurture and surround your children with love so they can blossom through the love that you unconditionally give them."

To me, working with Spirit is such a privilege and it is an amazing journey. Spirit is my life and even though it has been a hard life I would not know what to do without them. When I look back and I read people's letters and cards I think, WOW! I have helped a lot of souls move on and grow. This work has made me extremely humble. When it is my time to pass and I go over to the other side I will not be reincarnating back to the earth plane as I have been told I am to be a spiritual guide. 'A spiritual mentor' is what I look forward to calling myself. I will undertake an apprenticeship first and then be able to assist people on Earth who I am assigned to work with. I will help them to open the doorway to the other side just as those guides have helped me.

No doubt I will continue to question for the rest of my time here on Earth,

'Why me, why do I have this gift?' But with time and my trust in Spirit and the Universe, I know I will be able to fulfil my life's mission. The feelings of being two separate people will go and the struggle and disconnection will be gone and finally I will be whole and complete. Writing this book has been a huge part of my healing and as I read these final words during editing, my mother has come through and has said,

"It is all over now."

My Spirit guides have had the final say and in my head I hear the song,

"Time to Say Goodbye."

From left to right: Sue's daughters Sacha, Sarah, Samantha and granddaughter Janneke.

Grandson Khody, aged 5 years.

Steve and Sue.

A Message from Sue Murray

You Are A Lover Of Words.
One Day You Will Write a Book
People turn to you because you give voice to dreams,
Notice little things, and make otherwise impossible imaginings
appear real.
You are a rare bird, who thinks the world is beautiful
Enough to try to figure it out, who has the courage to dive into
Your wild mind and go swimming there.
Words do more than plant miracle seeds.
With you writing they can change the world.

A dear friend gave me this card ten years ago when she saw the serious dreamer in me. I treasured this card, enlarged it to A3 size, framed it, put it on my wall and thought maybe one day this is what I will do. Seven years later in a reading, Sue Nicholson told me, "One day you will work with me."

At the time I was heavily and passionately involved in initiating Movement Education for the Under Fives in New Zealand. I politely acknowledged her message and continued on with my work.

As does happen in life, the time comes when you realise a part of your journey is completed and there is something deep inside of you, gnawing at you, to come out.

When you begin working with Spirit you do take a huge leap in faith and trust. I thank my family for trusting, supporting and allowing me to follow a path that no-one besides Spirit knew where it was leading.

I thank my wonderful and enlightening friend Sue and also Spirit for having faith and trust in guiding me to discover my voice with this project. It is truly a magical and heartfelt place to be.

The longer I am fortunate to work with Sue and Spirit the more I expound,

How can you not believe?

Acknowledgements

To be where I am today has been an incredible journey but a journey I would not have been able to take if it hadn't been for the wonderful love, support and friendship that I have been honoured to receive.

Steve my soul mate, thank you for the undying love we share. You have certainly been tested many times and witnessed countless tears as I have struggled with the gift I have been blessed with. Your unwavering support of me touches the deepest part of my soul.

To my three beautiful daughters Samantha, Sacha and Sarah and my two wonderful grandchildren, Janneke and Khody, enjoy the gifts you each have and thank you for choosing me as your mother and grandmother. I could not have asked for more special people to come to me to share my life with.

Over my fifty three years I have met so many wonderful people. Thank you all for coming into my life and sharing our journeys together as we have all learnt so much from each other. Remember to walk your dream, to live it and to be you. Thank you to those people whose soul energies have given permission for their stories to appear in this book.

Ninox Productions, thank you for seeing the light that was within me and that I was capable of working on

Sensing Murder. You gave me the confidence to be all that I am and to bring it to the world. Cinna and Matt from Ninox Productions, thank you for always being so encouraging in so many aspects of the series and the supportive role you have shown me out side of work.

To Sue, 'my ghost writer' thank you for the amazing words and insight that you have put into this book as I know my vision from Spirit would not have become a reality without you. Your loyalty and trustworthiness this lifetime and also the previous lives we have journeyed together give me great strength and encouragement. I know this is only the start of what we are going to accomplish together. Thank you to Sue's family who in so many ways have supported us on this adventure.

Finally thank you to God and Spirit for giving me this gift. Even though at times it has been a difficult pathway to walk, I will not give up the contract.

God Bless you all